SCHOOL CHOICE AND THE QUESTION
OF ACCOUNTABILITY

School Choice and the Question of Accountability

The Milwaukee Experience

Emily Van Dunk and Anneliese M. Dickman

Yale University Press

New Haven & London

Copyright © 2003 by Public Policy Forum, Inc. Researching Community Issues.

Designed by James J. Johnson and set in Minion Roman types by Achorn Graphic
Services.
Printed in the United States of America by Sheridan Books, Ann Arbor, Michigan.

Library of Congress Cataloging-in-Publication Data

Van Dunk, Emily, 1966–
    School choice and the question of accountability : the Milwaukee experience / Emily
Van Dunk and Anneliese Dickman.
        p. cm.
Includes bibliographical references and index.
    ISBN 0-300-09942-8 (alk. paper)

    1. School choice—Wisconsin—Milwaukee—Case studies. 2. Educational
accountability—Wisconsin—Milwaukee—Case studies. I. Dickman, Anneliese, 1972–
II. Title.
    LB1027.9.V36 2003
    371.1'11'0977595—dc21

                                                        2003010389

A catalogue record for this book is available from the British Library.

The paper in this book meets the guidelines for permanence and durability of the
Committee on Production Guidelines for Book Longevity of the Council on Library
Resources.

10   9   8   7   6   5   4   3   2   1

Contents

Acknowledgments   vii

CHAPTER 1. The Limitations of Parental Accountability   1

CHAPTER 2. Parental Choice, Parental Power, and
Accountability   22

CHAPTER 3. The Response of Public Schools to
Competition   46

CHAPTER 4. What Parents Know: An Examination of
Informed Consumers   74

CHAPTER 5. Shopping for Schools   96

CHAPTER 6. Do the Dollars Follow the Child?   121

CHAPTER 7. Choice School Accountability: A Consensus
of Views   147

CHAPTER 8. Unleashing the Power of School Choice
Through Accountability   178

Notes   191

References   207

Index   217

Acknowledgments

We wish to acknowledge the advice, comment, and support of our mentors and bosses, former Public Policy Forum President David G. Meissner and current President Jeffrey C. Browne, who read and reread key portions of this manuscript and offered crucial suggestions and guidance. We want to recognize the support of Catherine A. Crother, whose title of office manager does not sufficiently cover all that she does to make our jobs easier. We were fortunate to work with a number of research assistants who took on the difficult task of assisting us in gathering and collecting data for two important chapters of this manuscript. Our onsite research assistant extraordinaire is Amy Schwabe, our interview team in Milwaukee included Jackie Champagne, Audra Grant, Jolene Jesse, Ann Lorman, and Dayna Velasco, and in Cleveland our interview team was directed by Ann Thornton, with the assistance of Tyree Ayers, Ronnie Dunn, Margaret Gerba, and Tobey Manns. Our parent-researchers were led by Tatyana Karaman, with the assistance of Darlene Budd, Elizabeth Clark, Yaasmeen Joseph, Berthina Joseph, Julie Siegel, and Maria Spirova. We thank John Witte and Paul Teske for their thoughtful edits and review of earlier versions of this manuscript. Without the financial support of the Joyce Foundation of Chicago and the Faye McBeath Foundation, the Richard and Ethel Herzfeld Foundation, and the Halbert and Alice Kadish Foundation, all of Milwaukee, this research would not have been possible. Finally, we thank Warren Chapman, former education program officer at the Joyce Foundation, whose intellectual vision and moral support allowed us the freedom to conduct objective research.

SCHOOL CHOICE AND THE QUESTION
OF ACCOUNTABILITY

CHAPTER ONE

The Limitations of Parental Accountability

In the end, every child in a bad situation must be given a better choice, because when it comes to our children, failure is not an option.
—PRESIDENT GEORGE W. BUSH (February 27, 2001)

Vouchers work. They don't hurt taxpayers and they encourage public schools to do better.
—JOHN NORQUIST, mayor of Milwaukee (January 30, 2001)

Choice . . . has the capacity all by itself to bring about the kind of transformation that, for years, reformers have been seeking to engineer in myriad other ways.
—JOHN CHUBB and TERRY MOE (1990)

Supporters of publicly funded private school choice are on a crusade to change education in the United States. They are struggling against a public school system that has a monopoly on education, assigning children to schools and controlling the money. Theoretically, because public schools dominate the provision of education, they have no incentive to improve. Abysmal proficiency levels and increasing dropout rates are met with a shrug and a sigh from some public school bureaucrats, who continue to request larger salaries and greater benefits despite declining student performance. Champions of school choice argue that what is needed to improve education is competition, along with the free market principles of supply and demand. The demand will come from parents who select schools based on their children's needs. Schools will either meet these needs or fail. Choice advocates are actively campaigning across the United States. Dozens and perhaps hundreds of organizations have emerged to lobby for choice, such as CEO America, the Council for American Private Education (CAPE), and the Black Alliance for Educational Options (BAEO).

On the other side of this issue we see matched intensity. Teachers' unions feel threatened by these efforts and are fighting against choice by matching and often surpassing the lobbying efforts of choice supporters. The stakes over control of education are so high and the struggle is so heated that we should anticipate no lessening of this controversy.

Lost in this battle is a discussion about how school choice should be implemented. This is unfortunate because, as with any major policy initiative, implementation matters. The major premise of school choice is that parents rather than the government or civil servants should be responsible for holding schools accountable. Under this scenario, the empowering of parents is the key to improving education. Through their vouchers parents, not elected officials or bureaucrats, will decide the fate of schools. A school's success will depend on its ability to capture enough of the market to remain open. School choice will break the monopoly on the control of public schools by opening the doors to competition. In those communities that allow it to prevail, competitive pressure, unlike traditional top-down bureaucratic accountability, will result in improved education.

This vision of parental choice assumes that parents' actions are a reliable accountability mechanism, one that will result in the demise of schools that cannot attract parents and the success of those that can. Three requirements must be met for parental accountability to work.

First, by choosing one school over another, parents send a message about what they believe is important for their children's education, and this message must be heard. Second, because parents' choices are backed by public money (vouchers), they will have a financial impact on both the gaining and losing schools. Third, when teachers and administrators recognize that they are in a competitive economic environment, they will try to gain market share. In the parental choice program, accountability depends on the link between schools and parents' actions. If this link is missing, parental empowerment and the promise of school choice are sorely diminished.

In the city of Milwaukee today, we have the nation's oldest and only large-scale voucher program, one that will test whether school accountability should rest solely in the hands of parents. After studying the Milwaukee voucher program for five years, the Public Policy Forum has found that the reality of parental choice accountability is falling far short of its promise. Relying on a detailed analysis of numerous datasets, including student enrollment, school characteristics, school startups and closures, parent, teacher, administrator, and taxpayer surveys, and school finances, we conclude that the system as it is currently designed does not accomplish what it is supposed to. Market forces do not or can not provide the rewards or exact the penalties expected. In real life, the school choices of parents do not result in accountability for schools. In the absence of effective accountability in a choice system, the inadequate public education that vouchers are supposed to improve may be replicated. The result, ironically, is that the very people choice schools are supposed to help—poor families—are betrayed, as are the taxpayers who are footing the bill.

The Promise of School Choice

School choice offers the promise of changing the face of education by placing the responsibility for school selection solely in the hands of parents rather than relying on a traditional system in which attendance zones are used to assign children to a public school and a limited choice is available only to parents with sufficient income. There are many forms of school choice, but the one that has captured the most attention and incited such controversy is that in which taxpayer-funded vouchers are provided to parents who choose to send their children to private school. Over the past half century, several prominent scholars have raised the idea that choice can improve our nation's public education system.

The economist Milton Friedman, writing in the 1950s and 1960s, promoted the idea of granting public money in the form of vouchers to parents to allow their children to attend any school they choose. Friedman believed that this system would encourage a variety of schools to open up to meet parent demand. He argued that the competition that would result among schools through a free market would be more efficient in meeting consumer demand than the current system of public education (1962: 89, 91). Almost forty years later, in an op-ed piece dated September 28, 2000, Friedman concludes that America needs school vouchers to improve society as a whole: "Failing schools are not the only reason for the parlous state of the inner cities, but they have played an important role. Far and away the biggest winner from an educational revolution would be society as a whole. A better-schooled work force promises higher productivity and more rapid economic growth." Friedman also claims that the evidence from Milwaukee and Cleveland supports this belief. In the same article Friedman notes, "I have nothing but good things to say about voucher programs, like those in Milwaukee and Cleveland, that are limited to a small number of low-income participants. They greatly benefit the limited number of students who receive vouchers, enable fuller use to be made of existing excellent private schools, and provide a useful stimulus to government schools. They also demonstrate the inefficiency of government schools by providing a superior education at less than half the per pupil cost."

A decade ago John Chubb and Terry Moe revived interest in the benefits of choice when they asserted that people should view choice as a panacea. They concluded that choice has the capacity by itself to bring about the kind of transformation in education that has not been possible with other reforms. They believed that by placing the responsibility for choosing in the hands of parents, we would see drastic improvement in education (1990: 217). Ten years later, in an opinion article in the May 9, 1999, edition of the *Washington Post*, Moe declared, "School vouchers offer an unprecedented opportunity to improve educational opportunities for children in our inner cities." He concluded by noting that he is convinced that the fight for inner-city vouchers will succeed. Vouchers, he believes, will bring new opportunities to millions of disadvantaged children and new vitality to urban public schools—which will have to perform at higher standards to keep students.

In two battles over choice that occurred in Michigan and California in the elections of November 2000, statements by choice supporters echoed the earlier promises proffered by Friedman, Chubb, and Moe. Dick DeVos, president of Alticor, Inc. (formerly known as Amway Corporation) and a financial supporter of the choice campaign in Michigan, maintained in a *Fox News* story of October 21, 2000, that in education just as in business, competition breeds improvement. DeVos declared, "When there is a choice, that's going to drive schools—public schools, charter schools, non-public schools, all of them—to be better, to earn that parent's choice." According to a report in *Education Week* on November 15, 2000, California's most prominent backer of vouchers, Timothy Draper, a Silicon Valley venture capitalist, funded the California voucher initiative to the tune of at least $23 million. A *Los Angeles Times* story on July 26, 2000, described Draper's view: that vouchers are a way for children to escape inferior neighborhood schools for the new, challenging private schools he believes entrepreneurs will open.

Need for Evidence

Although boldly stated, these promises are fundamentally about improving the education system through competition. Competition is created by placing accountability in the hands of parents, whose decisions have an impact on the school system. Bold claims regarding the impacts of choice can be substantiated only with hard evidence.

In the latter half of the 1990s and still today, scholars focused attention on analyzing the impact of private school choice programs (Greene, Peterson, and Du 1997; Green, Howell, and Peterson 1997; Howell and Peterson 2002; Levin 1998; Metcalf 1998a, 1999; Metcalf et al. 1998b; Peterson, Howell, and Greene 1999; Rouse 1998a, 1998b; Witte 1995, 2000). Most of this research centered on the specific achievement gains that private choice students experience over their counterparts in public schools. To date, however, there is uncertainty over just what these gains have been. The conflicting findings of these studies appear to be the result of using different controls or comparison groups and different methods of controlling for family backgrounds and student ability (Rouse 1998b). Whether one judges these studies to be methodologically sound often depends on one's support for school choice (see Fuller, January 22, 1997, *Wall Street Journal;* and Greene, March 17, 1998, *Milwaukee Journal-Sentinel*). The intensity of the debate has not diminished, as witnessed by the heated discussion over a voucher study released in August 2000. The study, as reported in the *New York Times* on September 15, 2000, was led by Paul E. Peterson and examined the impact of private vouchers in New York and Washington, D.C. Peterson concluded that there were significant test-score differences between African-American students who received vouchers and those who remained in public schools. The company that gathered the data, however, stated that these claims have been exaggerated.

More recent research has examined other effects of parental choice, particularly how choice as a market system affects the public school system. As Hess points out, one of the most commonly advanced arguments for school choice is that markets will force public schools to become more efficient and effective (Hess 2000: 3). Hoxby, however, examines school productivity, or achievement per dollar spent, in light of competition. She finds that public schools in Milwaukee, Arizona, and Michigan increased their productivity when they were exposed to competition from either vouchers or charter schools (2001). Hess and his coauthors examined the effects of vouchers on the public school systems in Milwaukee and Cleveland. Their studies produced mixed findings. In general, they found that competition had not had any systemic effects on teaching and learning (Hess 2000; Hess, Maranto, and Milliman 2000). Overall, the research on the impacts of vouchers on public school systems found that the financial formulas that accompany these policies protect the traditional public school districts from competition (Teske and Schneider 2000; Stuart-Wells 2000).

John Witte of the Robert M. LaFollette Institute of Public Affairs at the University of Wisconsin–Madison has written the most comprehensive work on the operation of a school voucher program. His book analyzed the early years of the Milwaukee Parental Choice Program (MPCP), from 1990 to 1995. The program provided private school vouchers to low-income families who resided in the city of Milwaukee. At the time of the study religious schools did not participate. There were only twenty-three voucher schools, and voucher recipients reached a maximum of 1,450, less than 1 percent of the total school enrollment in Milwaukee Public Schools (MPS). Witte was appointed by the Wisconsin Department of Public Instruction (DPI) to evaluate MPCP during the first five years of the program, comparing academic achievement, attendance, dropout rates, pupils suspended or expelled, and parental involvement. Witte consolidated his findings in *The Market Approach to Education: An Analysis of America's First Voucher Program* (2000).

Witte demonstrated that during the early years of MPCP, participants generally mirrored those in the public schools. As stated by Witte, "In nearly all respects, evidence from the Milwaukee voucher program leads to the conclusion that the creaming of students in limited and targeted voucher programs can be avoided" (Witte 2000: 73). He also found that choice student mobility was high and that the academic achievement of students receiving vouchers was not significantly higher than that of students who did not receive vouchers. In addition, he found that parents were satisfied with the program (2000).

Witte's research on the early years of vouchers provided critical evidence regarding who participates in the voucher program, why they participate, and what achievement gains, if any, voucher students have over their counterparts in public schools. The very early stages of the program, however, involved only four private schools. Because of this limitation many feel that there is a need to examine voucher programs that are much larger in scope (Moe 1995).

The Milwaukee Experience

Since Witte's analysis the voucher program in Milwaukee, now in its thirteenth year, has grown dramatically with the addition of private religious schools. The substantial size of Milwaukee's voucher program allows us to examine more fully the impact of vouchers on the education system by introducing competition.

There were 107 schools registered in the voucher program, with a full-time equivalent (FTE) enrollment of more than ten thousand students in the school year 2001–02. The current size reflects the inclusion of religious schools but is still below the statutory limit of 15 percent of

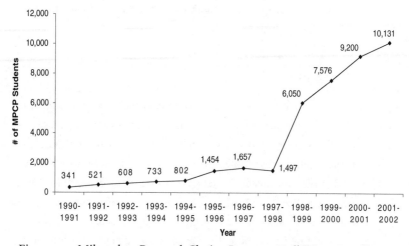

Figure 1.1. Milwaukee Parental Choice Program Full-Time Enrollment, 1990–91 through 2001–02

MPS enrollment, or about fifteen thousand students. Full-time enrollment in the voucher program has increased 500 percent since the inclusion of religious schools (fig. 1.1).

The ten thousand full-time students in MPCP surpasses the enrollment of 97 percent of the districts in the state of Wisconsin. Only eleven school districts in the state have more students than MPCP. The total MPCP enrollment also surpasses the national average public school district enrollment. According to data compiled by the National Center for Education Statistics (NCES), for 2000–01, the average U.S. school district enrollment was 3,179.

The voucher amount equals $5,553 per full-time student for the 2001–02 school year. The DPI estimates that in that year, $56 million was paid to private schools for the education of voucher students. This total amount exceeds the state aid received by 98 percent of the districts. According to the state Legislative Audit Bureau, the 2001–02 public voucher payment, in combination with the expenditures during the first ten years, totals $197 million.

The Setting

It was concern with the performance of Wisconsin's only large urban school district that moved Wisconsin policymakers to create the nation's first taxpayer-funded voucher program. During the deliberation over the creation of school choice in 1990 and its expansion in 1995, policymakers and pundits in Wisconsin decried the failing education system in Milwaukee. City business leaders supporting choice strongly believed that choice was needed to combat the failure of the Milwaukee Public Schools. Robert O'Toole, the chairman of the city's leading business group, declared his position in a *Milwaukee Sentinel* story on February 13, 1995: "The city's school choice program needs to be expanded because we are creating an army of illiterates with no skills."

Indeed, the Milwaukee public school district is one of the lowest-performing districts in Wisconsin. According to data collected by the DPI, Milwaukee ranked last out of forty southeastern Wisconsin school districts on four state standardized tests: third grade reading comprehension, and the fourth grade, eighth grade, and tenth grade knowledge and concepts tests. In addition, Milwaukee ranked last out of these forty districts in the percent of advanced placement tests passed and in the average composite score for the class of 1998 on the ACT college placement exam.

A number of proponents viewed vouchers as an opportunity to lift students, primarily minorities, out of one of the state's lowest-performing districts. Howard Fuller, distinguished professor at Marquette University, former MPS superintendent, and founder of BAEO, stated in a hearing before Congress in 1997, "I want poor black parents, poor parents of all colors for that matter, to have the same options that those of us with money have. It's the existence of an option outside [the public school system] that will help you fight to make the improvements inside." Milwaukee is also one of Wisconsin's few school districts in which minority students are in the majority. Approximately 80 percent of the district's students are nonwhite, with 62 percent African-American, 13 percent Hispanic, and 5 percent Asian.

Milwaukee is also one of the poorest districts in the state. Of the forty southeastern Wisconsin districts, MPS ranks first, at 77 percent, in percentage of students eligible for free or reduced-price lunch, last in property value per student, and last in earned income per household, at $27,624. Since 1988, the total equalized property value in Milwaukee has decreased by over $455 million, more than forty times that of the only other city to experience a loss in total value. Milwaukee also saw a population loss of 2.8 percent between 1990 and 2000. The city, therefore, has not seen an increase in per capita property value in the past decade, and at $26,575, the per capita property value is the lowest of sixty-seven southeastern Wisconsin municipalities.

Milwaukee was also one of the few districts in the state to offer public school choice to parents prior to the introduction of the voucher program. MPS had already abandoned the assignment of children to schools based solely on residence. Under an intradistrict public school choice program, Milwaukee parents participate in a three-choice selection process for either a citywide or regular public school. In addition, since the 1970s minority parents in the city have had the option to send their children to one of more than twenty suburban public school districts via an interdistrict integration program called Chapter 220. Suburban parents of nonminority children in participating districts can send their children to Milwaukee public schools under this same program. And since the voucher program began, other choice options, including charter schools and the statewide open enrollment program, have offered additional alternatives. Still, all of these choice programs require that public funds remain in public schools. School vouchers broke out of the confines of the public school system by challenging the public schools to compete with local private schools.

A Targeted Voucher Program

School vouchers in Milwaukee were supported by an odd coalition of conservatives and liberals. Jim Carl, writing about the creation of the Milwaukee voucher program, refers to these groups as unusual allies in their support for Milwaukee vouchers (1996). Wisconsin's Republican governor, Tommy Thompson, led the conservative supporters of school choice. The leading liberal champion of vouchers was Annette Polly Williams, state assemblywoman and representative from a majority African American district. For Williams the MPCP was born out of a long-term effort by the city's black parents to get adequate education for their children (1994).

Together these leaders assembled a diverse force that successfully lobbied and persuaded the state legislature to create a choice program in Milwaukee in 1990. Several years later this group gained strength from the business community, led by the Metropolitan Milwaukee Association of Commerce (MMAC), to lobby for an expansion of the program to include religious schools. In 1995 it was indeed expanded to include religious and nonreligious private schools.

The lobbying effort of the coalition resulted in a program that appealed to individuals who supported free-market concepts, as well as to others who supported allowing parents (in this case most were African American) to determine the best education for their children. It is not a universal voucher program. The Milwaukee choice program is limited by being aimed at a target market of urban, low-income, mostly minority families who are perceived by choice advocates as being trapped in educationally deficient public schools.

Why this targeted approach to educational choice rather than the broad free-market concept? It is clear that a targeted program was necessary to garner the requisite political support for school choice in Wisconsin. The Public Policy Forum's survey research indicated that 76 percent of taxpayers in the state supported choice. Of those surveyed, 23 percent supported choice only for low-income parents. Another 53 percent supported choice for all parents, regardless of income. With a reasonable margin for error, support for a broad choice program regardless of a parent's income was evenly split among taxpayers. At the same time, the survey showed that the African American community in Wisconsin did not support an unfettered market approach to education. For instance, when asked whether choice schools should be allowed to charge parents more in fees than the publicly financed voucher, only 43 percent of the African Americans said yes, compared to 71 percent of the whites (Van Dunk, Meissner, and Browne 1998). Overall support for choice was dependent on a combination of those who advocated vouchers for low-income families and those who backed vouchers for all parents. Moe reinforces this point in his detailed analysis of a public opinion survey on school vouchers across the U.S. (1995). He concluded that in order for voucher advocates to move their cause ahead, they must fashion proposals that take a centrist approach (2001: 371).

In other words, political conservatives who were mainly identified with a market approach to public education had to find allies among political liberals from low-income constituencies in Milwaukee. The latter were not necessarily market advocates. They were legislators and policymakers who in many cases felt that the traditional benefits of market economics had bypassed their constituents. They supported vouchers for low-income families as a solution to a failing urban public school system.

According to a state statute (Wisc. Stat. sec. 119.23), the program that passed in 1990 was as follows. Originally, voucher program eligibility was limited to pupils whose family income did not exceed 1.75 times the poverty level, as determined in accordance with criteria established by the director of the federal Office of Management and Budget. In addition, the total number of voucher recipients could not exceed 1 percent of the MPS district, or approximately one thousand students. No more than 49 percent of a participating private school's enrollment could consist of pupils receiving vouchers. Interested pupils had to submit an application to the participating private school on a form provided by the state. Schools that received more applications than they had seats available were to use a random selection process.

Schools that wanted to participate in the program had to so inform the DPI by May first of each year. Schools had to indicate the number of seats available for the coming year and were required to submit their plan for randomly selecting student participants if it became necessary (Mead 2000). Participating schools were required to provide at least 875 hours of instruction each year, including "instruction in a sequentially progressive curriculum of fundamental instruction in reading, language arts, mathematics, social studies, science and health." Schools were also required to meet at least one of the following standards:

1. At least 70 percent of the pupils in the program advance one grade level each year.
2. The private school's average attendance rate for the pupils in the program is at least 90 percent.
3. At least 80 percent of the pupils in the program demonstrate significant academic progress.
4. At least 70 percent of the families of pupils in the program meet parent involvement criteria established by the private school [Wis. Stat. sec. 119.23 (7a) 1990].

Milwaukee Vouchers and Accountability

The unusual coalition that came together to pass voucher legislation in Wisconsin had to deal with the issue of accountability early on. The two sides in the coalition did not believe equally that a free market should be the only source of accountability. The original bill, introduced by Representative Williams, cosponsored by thirty-six Republicans and eleven Democrats, and supported by Governor Thompson, did not include accountability guidelines. The Joint Finance Committee of the legislature, however, added minimal school performance standards and required an annual evaluation of the program. Because of these additions the original choice statute focused attention on evaluation.

In 1993, Wisconsin Act 16 amended the voucher program, beginning in the 1994–95 school year. The amendment increased enrollment from 1 percent to 1.5 percent of MPS enrollment, or about fifteen hundred students. In addition, the legislation allowed participating MPCP schools to increase voucher enrollment from 49 percent to 65 percent of their total students. As detailed in the *State of Wisconsin Budget in Brief, 1993–1995,* the governor's recommended budget also would have expanded accountability by requiring several measures recommended by Witte in his independent evaluation of the program. These recommendations were outlined in the executive budget and required that each private school participating in the MPCP (a) annually administer the state's third grade reading test and eighth and tenth grade attainment of knowledge tests to all pupils in the program and report the results to each pupil's parent or guardian; (b) have a formally constituted governing board; and (c) annually conduct an independent financial audit. As detailed in the *Summary of the Governor's Budget Recommendations, 1993–1995,* compiled by the Wisconsin Legislative Fiscal Bureau, the budget also directed the state superintendent to monitor school compliance with these requirements and prohibit continued participation in the program if any of the requirements were not met. The Joint Finance Committee deleted these provisions.

In the next budget cycle, 1995–97, the governor proposed to expand the MPCP by including religious schools and eliminating the voucher enrollment cap. The total number of voucher participants was increased to 15 percent of the MPS district, or approximately fifteen thousand students. The governor's proposal to expand choice eliminated the original provisions for DPI to conduct annual evaluations, and the governor did not reintroduce his earlier attempts to include accountability provisions in the legislation.

Representative Williams, however, along with seventeen other Democrats and nine Republicans, introduced legislation in 1995 that would have revived the accountability measures originally proposed by the governor. Assembly Bill 1008 required each private choice school to have a formally constituted governing board, a financial statement approved by its governing board, and staff grievance and parent complaint procedures. The bill also required each school to test its pupils in the third, fourth, eighth, and tenth grades.

Opponents of these accountability measures prevailed, and the bill was defeated in May 1996. At a public hearing, the opposition argued that the accountability standards would lead to significant state intrusion into private school operations. In statements made at the Wisconsin Assembly's hearing of the Committee on Urban Education in February 1996, other opponents argued that one cannot find a more regulated system than the public schools, yet this regulation has no correlation with student achievement. Proponents of the bill, meanwhile, argued that private choice schools must be held accountable for their expenditure of public funds.

The issue of accountability for voucher schools was not proposed again until the 1999–2000 legislative session, four years after the program's expansion was passed and one year after religious schools joined the program. Two Democratic senators from Milwaukee introduced Senate Bill 475. The bill again directed the DPI to extend its educational assessment program by requiring choice schools to test their pupils in the third, fourth, eighth, and tenth grades. The governing boards of the schools could adopt DPI's examinations or develop their own.

Schools would also be required to publicly list their governing boards and adopt Wisconsin's open records and meeting laws.

The statements made at the public hearing regarding Senate Bill 475 in March 2000 echoed the statements made in hearings held on choice in 1993 and 1995. Speaking for proponents of the bill, Representative Christine Sinicki, Democrat and former member of the Milwaukee School Board, argued that the bill would require MPCP schools to comply with the same standards of accountability as the public schools. The main argument was that if schools accept public money, they should be accountable to the public. Those arguing against this bill noted that it would seriously impair the ability of private schools to function as independent bodies. The arguments centered around the belief that this type of accountability was anathema to school choice supporters—because it undercut the very purpose of private education—to be responsible to private, individual concerns and not to the public at large. Moreover, the open records and open meetings laws would raise issues of excessive entanglement in religion. The bill failed in April 2000.

Most recently, the DPI requested in its 2001–03 budget that it administer standardized exams to pupils in the MPCP. The annual cost of administering these exams is estimated at $27 thousand. As reported in the *Milwaukee Journal-Sentinel* on February 14, 2000, school choice proponent Susan Mitchell, president of the American Education Reform Foundation, released a statement calling State Superintendent John Benson's ideas, "outrageous" and the "the latest chapter in DPI's long-standing effort to hamstring and ultimately stifle the program." This echoes earlier statements made by Mitchell in a *Milwaukee Journal-Sentinel* commentary entitled "How Choice Almost Died in Wisconsin" (September 6, 1999). Mitchell stated, "Too much regulation will prevent private school participation in publicly financed school choice programs, and opponents know it." Speaking for proponents of increased accountability, Chris Ahmuty of the American Civil Liberties Union of Wisconsin responded, "From our perspective, the most important issue is fairness. Why do some schools get to operate with a set of guidelines that would allow them to play fast and loose and operate in such a way that some parents and students won't be treated fairly. I think they have this fear that accountability will bring entanglement and bring down the whole program, and I just don't see that." In the end, the budget proposal submitted by Governor Scott McCallum in March included a provision that would cover the costs of schools that would like to *voluntarily* participate in the state's standardized exams. For those schools that did choose to participate, the results would be released only in the aggregate and not on an individual, school-by-school basis. This provision did not survive in the final budget.

The result is that accountability for the MPCP is solely based on the actions of parents. Milwaukee's program hinges on the link between what decisions parents make and the messages these decisions send to other schools. For this reason, Milwaukee allows us to see if this accountability system really works as it theoretically should, and it allows us to determine whether a system built on free market principles of parent accountability will achieve the primary goal of improving the educational quality of Milwaukee's schoolchildren.

The following chapters examine the adequacy of parent-based accountability for improving education by systematically examining the data on Milwaukee's school choice program. The book is organized around the three necessary components of parental accountability.

The first part of the book (chapters 2 and 3) concerns the first prong of accountability: the responsiveness of schools to parents. In our second chapter we examine the link between parents' decisions and the success or failure of voucher schools. At a minimum one would anticipate being able to identify good or bad schools by parents' movements into and out of schools. The data are clear, however: choice schools do not supply voucher seats in response to parents' desires, particularly at higher grade levels. The choice schools that have closed have not done so because of lack of parental demand. Because parents' choices are not driving schools to improve or to close, their actions will never lead to true accountability.

In our third chapter we further explore the effects of parents' choices on school decision making. This chapter looks at the link between parents' actions and accountability from the perspective of public schools. Are parents who are selecting private schools over public schools putting competitive pressure on the public schools? Are public schools responding by attempting to gain market share? We surveyed public school teachers in Milwaukee to sort out these possible effects. Our findings suggest that teachers are discussing the potential effects of competition and that public schools are making changes to retain and attract students. We find, however, that in MPS these changes are not related to the actual number of competing voucher schools nearby, but are more likely related to the threat of voucher competition even if no voucher schools are located nearby. Moreover, we found no evidence that the work activities of teachers have changed during this same time period.

Chapters 4 and 5 examine the second prong of accountability: whether parents are able to send a message to schools by acting to choose one school over another. Chapter 4 focuses on the amount of information parents have when making their schooling choices. Parental levels of knowledge about schools have traditionally been low. Choice should empower parents to seek out information on schools and select schools according to their needs. A pattern of low knowledge levels among choice parents would undermine the link between parents' actions and accountability, because it would indicate that parents' choices are not based on school factors. Addressing this issue of accountability requires understanding the level of information parents possess about the schools they chose. In addition, it requires directly examining the signals parents send when they select a school. Support for parental accountability hinges on the belief that parents will act as consumers by seeking out accurate information and by consistently choosing schools based on the factors they deem to be important. Our findings illustrate that choice parents possess limited knowledge about their schooling options.

The fifth chapter examines the experiences of parents as they choose schools. Using data from interviews with choice parents as a baseline, we sent a team of parent-researchers out to a representative sample of forty-one private choice schools. Their experiences help to highlight the knowledge of parents who are participating in the choice program. The greater the difficulty these parents encounter in obtaining information from schools, the less confident we are about linking accountability solely to the actions of parents. Our findings indicate that parents receive incomplete information from schools when shopping.

In the third section of the book (chapter 6), we discuss the third prong of accountability: Do the dollars follow the child? Thus, we examine how choice changes the structure of financing education. Public schools now compete with private schools for taxpayer dollars. How does this system work in Milwaukee? Do the actions of parents lead to clear winners and losers? How does the financial picture help us understand the link between parent actions and accountability? Our analysis suggests that the financial formulas that accompany the school choice program protect schools from financial harm, thereby muting the possible competitive effects of gaining or losing students.

Finally, our conclusion (chapters 7 and 8) focuses on a strategy for overcoming the missing link between parents' actions and accountability. Chapter 7 is intended to be a guide for policymakers and bureaucrats implementing a choice program in their state or district. Using data gathered through face-to-face interviews with hundreds of parents, teachers, and administrators and from telephone surveys with taxpayers, we outline a means for holding choice schools accountable that meets the needs of parents, respects the independence of private schools, and emphasizes the ultimate goal of parental choice: to improve the academic achievement of all children. Our concluding chapter makes a strong case for the need for strict performance accountability of all three types to allow choice to succeed in improving education.

Our intent is not to change the reader's position on choice by the findings laid out in this book. Instead, the information we share can help one understand how a system of education reform built on choice can best meet the stated goal: the improvement of education. Milwaukee is the best place in the United States to enlighten all of us interested in choice, and the time to begin this understanding is when one school is chosen over another.

CHAPTER TWO

Parental Choice, Parental Power, and Accountability

Milwaukee's private school choice program has no formal method of making schools accountable. There is no systematic reporting of test scores or any other outcome measurements, no accreditation system like those found among colleges or private elementary and secondary schools, no burdensome government requirements for teacher credentials or program uniformity. Instead, the Milwaukee program relies on the free market system of supply and demand, in which the consumers of education choose which schools thrive and which ones perish. In this case, the consumers are children and their parents. In theory, parents are the only people with the power to hold choice schools accountable. But how much information do parents really have about voucher schools in Milwaukee? What actions do they take with this knowledge? And are the actions of parents adequate to hold schools accountable for results that matter to parents and to taxpayers? These are critical questions in the absence of an outside accountability mechanism.

Because choice rests on free market enterprise rather than on formal measurements, a great deal of detective work is necessary to discover and interpret the actions of parents. In some ways, Milwaukee school choice creates a unique situation: in order to interpret parental actions, data would have to be collected systematically about those actions; yet, if such data collection were required, it would itself disturb the free market mechanism of accountability.

Our search for information began with the creation of an annual census of choice schools, and these data form the basis for the analysis in this chapter. In each of the past three years, the Public Policy Forum has surveyed choice schools to obtain basic information, including religious affiliation, school size, number of full-time teachers, the year the school was founded, tuition costs, transportation, enrollment periods, and number of voucher students. In order to obtain data from all participating schools, we sent multiple requests for the information, including letters and phone calls. We followed this with delivery of the request using certified mail and a messenger service. Finally, we visited each of the schools that had not supplied the information. The result was a 100 percent response rate. The data are supplemented with information published by the DPI on the number of participating students. The census is made available annually for the benefit of parents and others interested in the choice program and the schools that take part.

What Does the History of the Program Tell Us about Parents' Desires?

One of the notions of parental accountability is the belief that parents' actions lead to a competitive environment in which schools compete to meet parents' needs. The schools that meet those needs succeed, and those that do not, fail. By looking at characteristics of schools, we can gain some insight into whether this level of accountability exists in the choice program.

One means of doing this is to examine the fate of choice schools. How and when schools joined the program and why some schools left the program suggest the degree to which parents' actions have power over the schools. In 1990, the first year of MPCP, 7 private schools participated in the program, enrolling fewer than 400 students

in total. During the second year, 1991–92, 6 voucher schools participated. Five schools joined in 1992–93, bringing the number to 11 and
the enrollment to 608. In the fourth year, 1 school joined the program,
and in the fifth year, no additional schools joined, leaving the total at
12 schools and 802 students. Five schools joined the voucher program
in the sixth year, 1995–96, bringing the number of voucher schools to
17 and the number of voucher recipients to 1,454. In 1996–97, 7 schools
joined the choice program and 4 left, leaving 20 schools. In the eighth
year, 1997–98, 5 schools joined the voucher program and 2 left, for a
net of 23.

In 1998–99, the choice program expanded to include religious
schools, and 66 schools joined the choice program while 3 left. There
were 86 participating schools and 6,050 students. Over the next three
years, another 30 schools joined the program and 9 left, for a total of
107 schools and 10,321 voucher recipients in 2001–02.

In sum, over the past twelve years, 124 schools have been a part
of the school choice program, but as of 2001–02 there were just 107
active choice schools. What happened to the other 17 schools? Eight of
them closed. One changed its name and still exists as a school, but no
longer accepts voucher students. Another 4 left the choice program to
become Milwaukee charter schools: 2 chartered by the Common Council of the City of Milwaukee and 2 by MPS. Four schools vanished when
8 Catholic schools merged into 4 new schools. Mergers of Catholic parish schools have happened on the heels of mergers among Catholic parishes in Milwaukee. For example, if 3 Catholic parishes merged and 2
had schools, it became financially problematic to subsidize 2 separate
schools. Parish mergers are primarily a reflection of the loss of population in a city that lost 120,000 people from 1970 to 2000.

At the time each of these 17 schools ended their participation
in MPCP, they had a total of 955 voucher students enrolled (table 2.1).
The 4 schools that left MPCP to become charter schools enrolled a total
of 251 voucher students at that time. There were 259 voucher students

Table 2.1. School Closings and Withdrawals from MPCP

School	Status	Year Ended MPCP	Number of Full-Time Equivalent Voucher Recipients in Year Ended MPCP*
Exito Ed Center	Closed	1995–1996	113
Juanita Virgil	Closed	1990–1991	63
Milwaukee Prep	Closed	1995–1996	173
Neighborhood House	Closed	1998–1999	9
North Milwaukee Christian School (now called Grace Christian School)	No longer in MPCP but is in existence	1998–1999	7
SER Benito Martinez Academy	Closed	1996–1997	39
Waldorf School of Milwaukee	Closed	1995–1996	24
Bruce Guadalupe School	Charter through MPS	1998–1999	198
Downtown Montessori	Charter through city	1998–1999	6
Highland Community School	Charter through MPS	1996–1997	19
Khamit Institute	Charter through city	1998–1999	28
St. Lawrence and St. Matthew (now called Prince of Peace/ Principe de Paz)	Merged	1999–2000	117
Immaculate Conception and St. Augustine (now called St. Elizabeth Ann Seton Academy)	Merged	1999–2000	53.5
St. Vincent Palloti West and St. Vincent Palloti East (now called St. Vincent Palloti)	Merged	1999–2000	36.25
St. Barbara and Holy Spirit (now called St. Rafael the Archangel)	Merged	1999–2000	53
Gregory B. Flood Sr. Christian Academy	Closed	2000–2001	14
Zebaoth Learning Center	Closed	2000–2001	2
Total			954.75

* Some students register as part-time.

in the 8 Catholic schools that merged. The other 9 schools that once participated in choice enrolled 444 choice students when they left the program. These 9 schools give us insight into the role of parental actions in determining the fate of voucher schools.

In only one case over the past twelve years, that of the Waldorf School, was the closure of a choice school the direct result of parental action, but the parents who acted were not voucher parents; they were tuition-paying parents who left the school to form a new one. Waldorf School was in the choice program for four years, from 1992–93 to 1995–96. According to the *Milwaukee Journal-Sentinel* story on August 8, 1996, Waldorf was viewed as a success, and the closing came as a surprise to individuals in the community. In the year prior to closing, Waldorf had an enrollment of 130 students, 18 of which were voucher students. The closing of Waldorf was the result of competition. In an additional story appearing in the *Wisconsin State Journal* on August 9, 1996, all reports indicated that the school was soundly operating before closure. A group of parents left Waldorf to open Tamarack Community School. This resulted in a loss of both students and money for Waldorf. Whether the existence of the voucher program had any impact on why tuition-paying parents left the school is unclear. The reason given by parents for leaving Waldorf to open Tamarack school was that parents wanted to be more active in leadership and have more control over school finances. Parents who left and chose another school directly affected the operation of Waldorf. Yet the parents whose choice caused the closure of the school were not voucher parents. The number of voucher students at Waldorf increased during its final year of operation, from 18 to 24; total enrollment, however, dropped to 39.

The choices of parents did not factor in the decision of 8 out of the 9 schools to end their participation in MPCP. These 8 school closings were the result of financial mismanagement, the loss of a school director, or criminal charges brought against the school administrators.

Juanita Virgil Academy, one of the original 7 choice schools in

1990, did not finish its first school year. It got off to a rough start, as reported in the *Milwaukee Journal* on September 24, 1990. The first voucher payments to the school were delayed because the school was late in submitting enrollment information. By January, the school informed parents that it would be withdrawing from the choice program. In January 1991 the *Milwaukee Journal* reported that the voucher payments were not sufficient to cover the expenses of the school. Sixty-three full-time voucher students were enrolled when the school closed down. In 1998–99, the administrator who operated the academy opened up a new choice school, Texas Bufkin Academy, which continues to operate.

SER Benito Martinez Academy, also one of the original 7, remained open for seven years but closed after the 1996–97 school year, when it had 39 voucher students. The academy was both a choice school and an MPS partnership school, as are several choice schools that play double roles. Partnership schools have contracts with MPS to provide educational services to students at risk of dropping out of school, students with special needs, or adjudicated youth. These contracts are renewed each year if the school meets the obligations of the contract.[1] The closure of SER Benito Martinez as a choice school was not the result of declining voucher enrollment. Instead, closure was the result of a canceled partnership contract with MPS due to failure to meet MPS standards. In fact, during its final year, the academy's voucher student enrollment was at its highest ever, with 13 more choice students enrolled than in the previous year.

Exito Education Center opened in 1993–94 and closed three years later. The closing of Exito did not occur as a result of parents' actions. Rather, the closing came amid criminal charges against the school's administrator, who was accused of falsifying attendance records and issuing worthless checks as well as misdemeanor counts of possession of marijuana and drug paraphernalia. Exito falsely claimed to have had 113 voucher students in its final year of operation. If true, this would have been an increase of 98 students over the previous year. Although

the DPI had no authority to close a choice school, as highlighted in a *Milwaukee Journal-Sentinel* story on January 27, 1996, the department did send a letter to the director asking him to consider ceasing operations because of the criminal charges. The school did not reopen in 1996–97.

Milwaukee Preparatory Academy also closed in 1996, after the state charged the academy's founder with consumer fraud for lying about the age of some of the 173 choice students enrolled in the school so they would be eligible for reimbursement under the school choice program. The founder was sentenced to sixty-five months in prison in 1997.

Neighborhood House was in the choice program for one year, 1997–98. It had 9 voucher students. According to school administrators, the school decided to close after one year. Neighborhood House remains a daycare center but does not provide educational services to grade school children. The decision to close was apparently not because of a loss of parents.

North Milwaukee Christian School joined the choice program in 1998–99 but stopped participating after one year. The school had 7 voucher students in that year. The actions of voucher parents apparently did not influence the closing of this school; it still exists as a private school, though the name has been changed to Grace Christian School, and it no longer accepts voucher students. The administrator who spoke to us gave no reason for the school's decision to leave the program.

Two more voucher schools joined the choice program in 2000–01 and closed down at the end of that school year. Zebaoth Learning Center had a total of 2 voucher children in their kindergarten-only school. According to the church pastor, the school director moved away at the end of the school year, and they did not have another director in their church to keep the school running. Gregory B. Flood Sr. Christian Academy had 14 voucher students enrolled in its only year of operation.

Because repeated attempts to contact the school were unsuccessful, no reason for closure of this school could be obtained.

The brief history of these 9 choice schools demonstrates that the actions of parents thus far have been a weak means for holding choice schools accountable in Milwaukee. The evidence over twelve years of choice is that parental decisions to leave one school and attend another had a very limited impact, or no impact, on these school closings. Indeed, of 17 school closings or withdrawals from the program, just 1 was caused by parental choice, and those who so chose were not voucher recipients but tuition-paying parents who, ironically, may have abandoned the school partly because it was popular with voucher parents. In fact, the number of voucher students in that school, as in all of the schools that have closed, increased in their final year of operation.

What Does School Enrollment Tell Us about Free Market Accountability?

Although we do not see evidence that voucher parents' decisions affect the closing of schools, perhaps the impact of parents on the enrollment in schools in the choice program is easier to observe. Again, parental choice theory suggests that parents will flock to good schools and leave or never attend poorly performing schools. One way to look at this phenomenon is to examine the increase in enrollment.

The voucher program can be divided into two time periods. In the first period, from 1990 through mid-1998, choice students were limited to fewer than 25 nonsecular schools, and the majority of students attended just 1 of 3 schools. In the second period, from 1998–99 to the present, more than 80 schools joined the choice program and voucher student enrollment matched this dramatic increase. Because choice in the early years involved relatively few students and schools, we focus on the latter period.

Table 2.2. Increase in Full-Time Voucher Recipients, 1998–99 to 2000–01

School	Increase in Students (N)	Increase in Students (%)
Early View Academy of Excellence	207	269
Messmer High School	177	114
Salam School	147	344
St. Anthony School	132	77
Urban Day School, Inc.	121	30
Marva Collins School	100	71
Holy Redeemer Christian Academy	98	40
Harambee Community School	91	38
Woodson Academy	82	42
Milwaukee Multicultural Academy	79	400

Since the expansion of the program in 1998–99, 10 schools have seen a decrease in voucher student enrollment while 66 have seen an increase. Early View Academy of Excellence, located on Milwaukee's North Side, gained the most enrollment, increasing by 207 students (269 percent) from the fall of 1998 to the fall of 2000. Messmer High School also added a large number of students, more than doubling the number of voucher recipients to a total of 331 students in fall 2000. Milwaukee Multicultural Academy added 79 voucher students over this three-year period, a 400 percent increase. Table 2.2 lists the ten schools with the greatest growth in number of voucher students since 1998–99.

Can we conclude that schools that lost voucher students are less desirable to parents than schools that gained voucher students? According to the market theory of parental choice, we should be able to conclude this. Nevertheless, our research indicates that we cannot possibly make that conclusion. We found that one weakness in using an increase in voucher student enrollment as a measure of accountability is that total school enrollment does not necessarily correlate with the number of voucher students in a school. Of the 21 schools with 300 or

Table 2.3. Total Enrollment and Percentage Choice Enrollment in Largest Choice Schools

School	Enrollment	Students Receiving Vouchers (N)	Students Receiving Vouchers (%)
Pius XI High School	1,555	72	5
Marquette University High School	994	21	2
Urban Day School, Inc.	600	526	88
Divine Savior Holy Angels	570	10	2
Messmer High School	502	331	66
St. Gregory the Great	470	20	4
Mother of Good Counsel	458	106	23
St. Margaret Mary School	457	57	12
St. Sebastian School	444	74	17
St. Roman Parish School	438	31	7
St. Veronica School	418	20	5
Harambee Community School	406	329	81
St. Anthony School	398	304	76
St. Joan Antida High School	392	169	43
Holy Redeemer Christian Academy	388	344	89
Milwaukee Montessori School	322	17	5
Prince of Peace/Principe de Paz	306	208	68
Early View Academy of Excellence	303	284	94
Woodson Academy	301	278	92
Marva Collins Preparatory School	300	240	80
Learning Enterprise High School	300	156	52

Note: Boldface indicates schools with <25% voucher enrollment.

more students, 10 have less than 25 percent of their enrollees receiving vouchers. The largest schools, Pius XI and Marquette University High School, have 5 percent and 2 percent voucher enrollment, respectively (table 2.3). Tuition-paying parents seem to choose these schools in greater numbers than voucher parents. Indeed, for all the schools in the program, there is no statistically significant correlation between total school enrollment and the number of voucher students. In fact, MPCP may generate adverse selection: only those schools that cannot fill their

Table 2.4. Top Ten Increases in Total Enrollment and Voucher
Student Enrollment, 1998–99 to 2000–01

School	Total Enrollment Increase
Early View Academy of Excellence	200
Messmer High School	142
Salam School	159
St. Anthony School	124
Urban Day School, Inc.	102
Marva Collins Preparatory School	119
Holy Redeemer Christian Academy	102
Harambee Community School	51
Woodson Academy	77
Milwaukee Multicultural Academy	70

School	Voucher Enrollment Increase
Early View Academy of Excellence	207
Salam School	147
Messmer High School	177
St. Anthony School	132
Marva Collins Preparatory School	100
Urban Day School, Inc.	102
Holy Redeemer Christian Academy	102
Parklawn Christian School and Preschool	92
Woodson Academy	77
Milwaukee Multicultural Academy	70

capacity with tuition-paying parents may seek voucher students. Therefore, growth in voucher student enrollment may be more a measure of
opportunity—the fact that seats are available—than a measure of school
desirability.

We found, however, that dramatic increases in total student
enrollment in participating schools over the past three years do appear
to be the result of increases in voucher students rather than in tuition-
paying students. The schools having the largest increases in enrollment

are also those schools that have gained the most voucher students. Table 2.4 lists the top 10 schools that have increased their enrollment from 1998–99 to 2000–01 and the top 10 schools that have increased voucher student enrollment during this same time period. Nine of the 10 schools that gained the most enrollment are also in the top 10 for increases in voucher students. Only Harambee Community School and Parklawn Christian School do not fit this description.

Searching for the Link between Accountability and Supply and Demand

From this perspective, it appears that looking at total enrollment and voucher student increases leads to possibly different conclusions regarding the meaning of parental actions. Why would a school that attracts hundreds of tuition-paying parents attract only a handful of voucher parents when other schools are able to dramatically increase their enrollment by attracting voucher parents? One reason may be a tenuous link between the demand for and availability of voucher seats. Put differently, perhaps schools that can attract a sufficient number of tuition-paying students can limit the number of voucher seats available and still thrive, while schools that cannot fill their seats with tuition-paying students must be willing to take as many voucher students as they can recruit. If this is the case, changes in voucher enrollment tell us nothing about voucher school quality or desirability.

Over the past three years, the schools with the largest number of voucher students for the most part gained even more and therefore remained among the largest. As table 2.5 shows, only 2 schools have moved out of the top 10 largest voucher schools in the past three years. Saint Leo Catholic School lost 43 voucher students and moved from sixth largest to thirteenth. The other school to move off of the top 10 list is Blessed Trinity, which closed at its previous location on the North

Table 2.5. Top Ten Schools Enrolling Voucher Students, 1998–99 to 2000–01

1998–99		1999–2000		2000–01	
School	MPCP Enrollment	School	MPCP Enrollment	School	MPCP Enrollment
Urban Day	401	Urban Day	478	Urban Day	526
Holy Redeemer	259	Harambee	297	Holy Redeemer	344
Harambee	247	Holy Redeemer	268	Messmer	331
Woodson	196	Messmer	257	Harambee	329
St. Leo	195	St. Anthony	234.5	St. Anthony	304
St. Anthony	184	St. Leo	219.6	Early View	284
St. Adalbert	180	Woodson	213	Woodson	278
St. Rose	176	Blessed Trinity	209	Marva Collins	240
Blessed Trinity	168	St. Adalbert	205.5	St. Adalbert	231
Marva Collins	158	Prince of Peace	180.5	Prince of Peace	208

Side of Milwaukee and reopened as Messmer Preparatory School on Milwaukee's near East Side. The school lost 52 voucher students in this move and is now the eighteenth largest voucher school.

Mirroring this trend is the consistency of schools at the bottom of the list for voucher student enrollment. Eight of the schools enrolling the smallest number of voucher students remained in this category for the past three years.

We also noticed that the large number of voucher schools somewhat overshadows the fact that most voucher recipients were concentrated within a few schools, as illustrated in table 2.6. Choice for the first eight years largely involved just 3 private schools: Bruce Guadalupe, Harambee, and Urban Day. Seven out of 10 voucher students in the first five years attended one of these 3 voucher schools. In years six through eight, half of the voucher students attended these 3 schools. After the expansion of the voucher program to include religious schools, in the 1998–99 and 1999–2000 school years, 50 percent of participating voucher students attended 18 schools. In 2000–01, 50 percent of voucher students attended 19 schools. One-third of all voucher recipients attend just 10 choice schools.

After noticing these two trends—that the schools with the largest and smallest numbers of voucher students tend to remain constant and that the voucher students tend to remain clustered in a few schools—we began to question whether supply-and-demand-driven school accountability holds true for Milwaukee's choice program. Are the schools that experienced the greatest *growth* in enrollment of voucher students the best schools? Are the schools with the largest *numbers* of voucher students the best schools? Are the 19 schools that *enroll 50 percent or more* of the voucher students the best schools? Are the schools with the largest number of tuition-paying students the best schools? While any of these scenarios may be the case, voucher parent demand does not seem to be driving increases or decreases in voucher seats.

Table 2.6. Collective Enrollment of 50% of Voucher Students, 1998–99 to 2000–01

1998–99			1999–2000			2000–01		
School	MPCP Enrollment	Cumulative Percent	School	MPCP Enrollment	Cumulative Percent	School	MPCP Enrollment	Cumulative Percent
Urban Day School	405.5	7	Urban Day School	478	6	Urban Day School	526	6
Holy Redeemer Christian Academy	245.6	11	Harambee Community School	297	10	Holy Redeemer Christian Academy	344	9
Harambee Community School	238.25	15	Holy Redeemer Christian Academy	268	14	Messmer High School	331	13
Woodson Academy	196.3	18	Messmer High School	257	17	Harambee Community School	329	17
St. Leo Catholic Urban Academy	188	21	St. Anthony School	237.5	20	St. Anthony School	304	20
St. Anthony School	171.75	24	St. Leo Catholic Urban Academy	219.6	23	Early View Academy of Excellence	284	23
St. Rose Catholic Academy	171	27	Woodson Academy	213.4	26	Woodson Academy	278	26
St. Adalbert School	170.25	30	Blessed Trinity Catholic School	209	29	Marva Collins Preparatory School	240	29

School	Value	Rank	School	Value	Rank	School	Value	Rank
Blessed Trinity Catholic School	165	32	St. Adalbert School	205.5	31	St. Adalbert School	231	31
Messmer High School	154.5	35	St. Rose Catholic Academy	179.5	34	Prince of Peace/Principe de Paz	208	33
Marva Collins Preparatory School	139.75	37	Marva Collins Preparatory School	178	36	Salam School	189	35
Resurrection Catholic Academy	139.25	39	Early View Academy	166	38	St. Rose Catholic Academy	189	38
St. Catherine School	127.25	42	St. Catherine School	165	41	St. Leo Catholic Urban Academy	176	39
Believers in Christ Christian Academy	126.3	44	Resurrection Catholic Academy	147.5	43	St. Catherine School	174	41
St. Philip Neri Catholic School	110.5	45	Salam School	146	44	St. Joan Antida High School	169	43
Mount Calvary Lutheran School	109	47	Believers in Christ Christian Academy	142.4	46	Resurrection Catholic Academy	160	45
Agape Center of Academic Excellence	101.3	49	St. Philip Neri	123	48	Believers in Christ Christian Academy	158	47
St. Martini Lutheran School	96.3	51	Mount Calvary Lutheran School	118	50	Messmer Preparatory Catholic School	157	48
						Learning Enterprise High School	156	50

Table 2.7. High School Total Enrollment and Voucher Student Participation, 2000–01

School	Type	Enrollment	Voucher Students	Change in Voucher Students, 1998–2000
Pius XI High School	Coed Catholic	1,555	72	43.5
Messmer High School	Coed Catholic	502	331	176.5
Marquette University High School	All boys Catholic	985	21	10
St. Joan Antida High School	All girls Catholic	392	169	74.5
Divine Savior Holy Angels High School	All girls Catholic	570	10	7
Learning Enterprise High School	Coed Nonreligious	300	156	79
Grandview High School	Coed nonreligious	223	20	3

High school enrollment figures provide an example of the inadequacy of supply and demand. As table 2.7 shows, seven Milwaukee high schools accept voucher students. Voucher enrollment growth since 1998–99 varied from 3 in Grandview High School to 176.5 in Messmer High School. Messmer enrolled 331 voucher students, representing 66 percent of the school's total enrollment. Should we conclude that because voucher parents are flocking to Messmer this is the best voucher high school? Maybe so, but the actions of voucher parents are insufficient for drawing this conclusion if schools are using criteria other than parental demand for determining the number of voucher seats available. For instance, only 21 seats were available to voucher parents who desired the elite prep school education offered by Marquette University High School. Marquette's total enrollment was 985, meaning that voucher students represented 2 percent of the school's population. If supply is limited, then demand is constrained, and if demand is constrained then

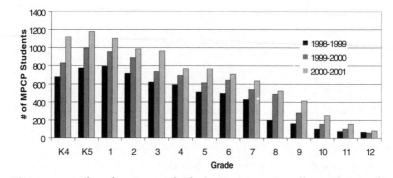

Figure 2.1. Milwaukee Parental Choice Program Enrollment by Grade (September Headcount)

it does not say anything about quality. If we know nothing about quality, we have no accountability.

Further evidence that supply and demand may not be mechanisms for accountability becomes apparent when we examine the number of voucher seats by grade level. Voucher schools have predominantly served lower grade students for the twelve-year history of the program. As figure 2.1 illustrates, children receiving vouchers in both four- and five-year-old kindergarten (K4 and K5) outnumbered voucher high school students by a ratio of 2.5 to 1. There are currently 2,295 kindergartners in 81 schools receiving vouchers compared to 888 high school students in 8 schools. Why don't more high schools participate? Do parents of high schoolers desire voucher schools at a much lower rate than parents of kindergartners? Perhaps, but it seems more likely that high schools have chosen not to participate or offer additional seats to voucher students for other reasons.

We wanted to know what those reasons might be. Perhaps the city has fewer children of high school age. We looked at total enrollment in the city and found that the number of students in Milwaukee does not drop as grade level increases as dramatically as the number of voucher students as grade level increases. For example, in the city of

Milwaukee in 1999–2000 there were 10,775 nine-year-olds attending both public and private schools. The number of sixteen-year-olds totaled 8,345, a difference of 23 percent. The comparable grade level in MPCP would be third or fourth grade for nine-year-olds, and tenth or eleventh grade for sixteen-year-olds. In MPCP that same year, the number of nine-year-olds totaled 717 and of sixteen-year-olds totaled 129, a difference of 82 percent. MPCP schools enroll proportionately fewer high school students than do city schools on the whole.

Another way to represent this pattern is to examine whether the supply of voucher seats by grade is sufficient to accommodate currently enrolled students as they move up. Ideally, this analysis should be done with individual-level data; however, those data are not available to researchers. As an alternative, we look at the aggregate data and ask whether it appears that enough seats are being added to accommodate students as they advance to the next grade level. This assumes that students currently in the voucher program want to remain in the program at the next grade level. For example, if there were 677 K4 students in 1998–99, there would need to be at least 677 seats in K5 the following year.

We found that the number of voucher seats in grades one through six is sufficient to accommodate all students enrolled in 1998–99 as they progress. Starting at the seventh grade, however, there are not enough seats to accommodate the sixth grade students of 1999–2000. This pattern exists for eighth through twelfth grades as well.

Again, this suggests there may be a missing link between supply, demand, and accountability. But could it be that parents are selecting private schools at a much lower rate in high school than in elementary school? If so, this would be an example of supply responding to demand and would support the idea that parents are holding schools accountable. If this were true, however, we would expect to see similar trends in total private school enrollment by grade, including enrollment by tuition-paying students. The data do not reflect this trend. Overall,

27 percent fewer sixteen-year-olds than nine-year-olds are enrolled in private schools in Milwaukee. That difference is significantly smaller than the 82 percent found for voucher students alone.

One possible explanation may be that the voucher schools that serve the primary grades may be better schools than the voucher schools that serve students in high school. Parents who receive vouchers may be taking their children out of private schools when they reach middle and high school and may be choosing better quality public schools. If this is the case, however, we cannot explain why voucher parents would view private schools participating in MPCP differently than do tuition-paying parents.

Our examination of the available data leads us to conclude that one of the reasons for the weak link between accountability and supply and demand in the choice program is that most MPCP parents were already enrolled in private school before receiving a voucher.[2] With MPCP came an expectation that new schools would open to meet the demand created by voucher students. Therefore, we should see an associated increase in private school enrollment. In reality, there was no new growth in private school enrollment. The number of Milwaukee children enrolled in private school declined dramatically between 1965 and 1977. Since then the number has risen somewhat, but for the 1990s, the time period spanning the voucher program, there has been a slight decline. As figure 2.2 highlights, even the inclusion of religious schools in the choice program in 1998–99 did not result in a corresponding boost in the number of city children attending private school.

Part of the trend in private school enrollments can be explained by examining where voucher students were enrolled before they became voucher students. On the application form, potential MPCP students must indicate where they attended school the previous year. In 1998–99, the first year of expansion, 62 percent of MPCP students were already enrolled in private schools the previous year. Of these, 39 percent were attending private schools either as tuition-paying students or as recipi-

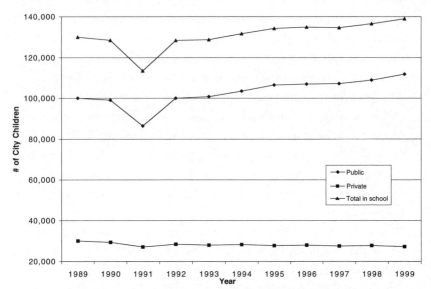

Figure 2.2. Number of City Children Attending Public and Private School, 1989–99

ents of private scholarships. Another 23 percent had been receiving vouchers to attend private schools. Less than one quarter of the new students had been enrolled in MPS the previous year.

In 1999–2000, the second year of expansion, this pattern was repeated. A total of 60 percent of MPCP students indicated that they were voucher students the previous year, and another 3 percent had been enrolled in private schools as either tuition-paying or scholarship students. One quarter of the students were previously enrolled in MPS.

The most recent data, from 2000–2001, show 64 percent of MPCP students were attending private schools as voucher students the previous year and another 3 percent were attending private school as tuition-paying or scholarship students. Twenty-one percent, the lowest percentage in three years, had been attending MPS the previous year (figure 2.3).

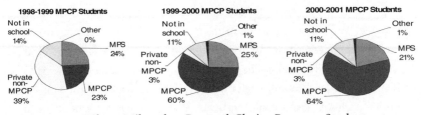

Figure 2.3. Where Milwaukee Parental Choice Program Students Were Enrolled the Previous School Year

What does this tell us about supply and demand? For one thing, it suggests that most voucher parents had already chosen not to send their children to public school before they received a voucher. The voucher program neither empowered these parents to make their choice nor created greater demand for private schools. When supply is not responsive to demand it becomes difficult, if not impossible, to use supply and demand of vouchers as a mechanism for holding schools accountable.

The flip side of demand for a school is exit from it, and so we look at mobility in the choice program as a potential way to understand the message parents send when they leave a school. Although 6,130 students participated in MPCP in 1998–99, just 4,573 of them continued their participation in the program in 1999–2000. On an aggregate level, this means that nearly 1,500 students left the program.[3] This represents an aggregate mobility rate of 25 percent. This pattern was repeated the next year. Of the approximately 8,000 MPCP students in 1999–2000, only 5,700 continued the program in 2000–01, a mobility rate of 28 percent.[4] Mobility in MPS during this same period was 22 percent for elementary, 21 percent for sixth through eighth grade, and 25 percent for high school.

If we knew which schools these children were leaving, parental accountability could be improved. As noted in a Legislative Audit Bureau report of 2000, "Although frequent pupil mobility among schools is generally perceived to be undesirable, one purpose of MPCP is to provide families with the opportunity to transfer between schools to seek the best education for their children. As a result it is not clear whether mobility among schools indicates program success or failure." If individual-level mobility data were available it would be a means for holding schools accountable. Instead, we know only that schools must be losing choice students and replacing them with new choice students.

Parental Choice in the Education Marketplace

In a true education marketplace, pure freedom of parental choice should reveal which schools are good and drive bad schools out of business. If limits are put on parents' movements, however, accountability based on parents' actions is much harder to envision. In the worst case, gains or losses of voucher students mean virtually nothing, making it difficult to hold choice schools accountable using parental action alone. One such limit on parents' choices is when there is only a weak link between demand and supply. Parents may select schools, but the reasons for their choices are more likely related to the supply of seats available rather than the parents' demand. This is problematic because an inelastic supply leads to a constrained demand. A constrained demand cannot tell us anything, good or bad, about a school's desirability.

The data provide evidence that the supply of seats might not necessarily correlate with demand. We know that schools leaving the choice program do not do so because voucher parents are not choosing them; more than 440 voucher students have chosen schools that failed to participate in the program the following year. We know that many large and popular private schools have relatively few voucher students, suggesting that some schools may cap the number of voucher seats, choosing instead to maintain their tuition-based enrollment. We know that the growth in the number of schools participating is not due to parents demanding more choice; although 103 schools currently accept vouchers, most voucher students attend one of only 19 schools. We know that choice schools enroll proportionately fewer of Milwaukee's high school students than other private schools in the city, suggesting that the low number of high school voucher students is not indicative of low parental demand for private high schools. We know that if voucher seats were available in the higher grades, many parents likely would continue to choose voucher schools; between ages nine and sixteen, voucher students leave the program at a rate nearly four times greater than students leave private schools on the whole. We know that when the program expanded to include religious schools, two-thirds of the new voucher students had attended private school the previous school year, while less than a quarter of the new voucher students had been in MPS the year before, indicating that the program's growth was not solely the result of public school parents' demands. Finally, we know that each year at least one quarter of voucher students do not use a voucher the following year and are replaced in even greater numbers by new voucher students, resulting in parent movement that does not hold individual schools accountable.

Milwaukee's choice program is based on the premise that parents' actions will lead to an accountability system in which good schools succeed and poor schools fail. The data available offer no evidence that this is or is not happening thus far in Milwaukee. The increase or decrease of voucher students tells us nothing about school quality because choice schools do not supply voucher seats in response to parents' demands, particularly at higher grade levels. Parents' choices do not drive schools to improve or close. In Milwaukee, no one can claim that parents hold voucher schools accountable: there is no evidence whether they do or do not.

CHAPTER THREE

The Response of Public Schools to Competition

To this point we have been examining whether private voucher schools are held accountable by the actions of parents. One of the most debated issues surrounding school choice, however, is its impact on public schools. Because the vast majority of U.S. students, including those in Milwaukee, attend public school, one of the most significant issues raised by school choice is whether the actions of parents have competitive effects on public schools.

Under the market theory adding competition to the public education monopoly should provide an incentive for public schools to improve in order to gain or retain market share. In this chapter we test this theory by examining the impacts of competition on public school teachers and schools in Milwaukee. We evaluate changes in both school inputs and outputs because schools may quickly adopt changes in response to competition but there may be a time lag in the effect of these changes on achievement outcomes (Hess 2000). To examine changes in school inputs, in the fall of 2000 we surveyed 457 MPS teachers to determine if their teaching activities or their schools' climates had changed since the expansion of Milwaukee's private school choice program in the 1998–99 school year. In addition, we examined school outputs by using performance data of MPS schools to measure the impacts of competition on changes in student achievement.

Our initial findings suggest that teachers are discussing the potential effects of competition and that many schools are making changes to retain and attract students. We also find, however, that these changes are not related to the existent level of voucher competition facing any one school, as measured by the number of nearby voucher schools, but may more likely be related to the potential threat of competition—even if there are not yet any voucher schools nearby. Changes in school performance do not seem to be tied to existent competition either.

The Impact of Choice on Public Schools

In chapter 2, we found that the actions of parents do not appear to hold voucher schools accountable; in theory, the actions resulting from these parents' choices should also affect the public school system. One of the most commonly advanced arguments for school choice is that competition will force public schools to become more efficient and effective (Hess et al. 2000). So far, the results of research on the effects of competition on public schools have varied. Hoxby (1998, 2003) and Dee (1998) find significant competition-induced improvements in public schools. Armour and Peiser (1997, 1998) and Rofes (1998) find improvements in some cases, while Wells (1998) and Gorard (1997) find no significant effects. Smith and Meier (1995) and Geller et al. (2000) find negative effects.

In addition, Hess and his coauthors find mixed results after examining the effects of choice on the public school systems in Milwaukee, Cleveland, and Arizona. In general, they find that competition has not had any systemic effects on teaching and learning. Their evidence does suggest, however, that competition was causing subtle changes by spurring on reform and empowering innovative teachers and administrators (Hess 2000; Hess et al. 2000; McGuinn and Hess 2000). Recent work by Teske et al. (2000) echoes these findings. These authors examine the impact of charter schools on five urban school districts and find that, owing to a variety of factors, most districts are shielded from the direct impact of charter schools, although some individual principals do respond to competitive pressure from charter schools.

Our research focuses on the impacts of increasing competition on public school teachers and schools in Milwaukee, where almost 10,000 students receive vouchers to attend private school.

Milwaukee Teacher Survey

In September 2000 we sent a four-page, sixty-five-item mail survey containing both open- and closed-ended questions to 2,500 MPS teachers at their schools. Before mailing, the survey was pretested on a focus group of current and former public school teachers. We obtained from the DPI a database of MPS teachers that includes information about the teacher's school, grade level, months of experience, gender, and race. Because we were interested in the relations between competition and changes in teachers' work lives, we chose to survey MPS teachers whose teaching activities were most likely to reflect the influence of competition. In other words, we chose teachers whose work lives were the least likely to change as a result of other influences, such as gaining greater professional confidence. Teachers who have made it through the typical turnover cycle—those with at least seven years of teaching experience—were deemed to fit this requirement. To ensure a random sample within these criteria, we used a random number generator to assign identification numbers to each of the 2,917 MPS teachers with at least seven years of experience, and we selected ID numbers 1 through 2,500 to be surveyed.

An additional mailing of a reminder postcard followed the survey, and we received 457 survey responses by our deadline. Fourteen respondents had altered the survey such that the ID number was no longer legible. We could not link these responses to the DPI database

Table 3.1. Representativeness of Survey Respondents

Teachers with at least seven years experience	Respondents (% of total survey sample) (N) (%)		MPS teacher population (% of total MPS teacher population) (N) (%)	
All	457	(100)	2,917	(100)
With demographic data	443	(97)	2,917	(100)
Female	333	(73)	2,040	(70)
African American	40	(9)	555	(19)
Hispanic	17	(4)	109	(4)
White	384	(84)	2,222	(76)
High school grades	105	(23)	768	(26)
Elementary and middle school grades	328	(74)	2,051	(70)
Central administration	10	(2)	98	(3)

Note: Percentages may not total 100% due to rounding.

and therefore have no demographic or school data for those fourteen, giving us a final response rate of 18 percent. Of the respondents in the 443 usable surveys, ten teachers work in MPS central administration and not in a particular school. The total number of schools represented by the responding teachers is 134, with an average representation of 3.2 teachers per school. The maximum number of teachers representing one school is 11, and the minimum is 1. As shown in table 3.1, except for an underrepresentation of African American teachers, the demographics of the sample of surveyed teachers is representative of the MPS teacher population with at least seven years of experience. The sample has a margin of error of 4.8 percent with 95 percent confidence.[1]

To measure change over time, we asked teachers to compare their current situation with a past one. But instead of asking teachers to compare aspects of their jobs now with aspects from a specific previous school year, which could be difficult to pinpoint in a teacher's memory, we asked them about changes in their jobs over the past two school years or so.[2] We were interested in the two school years previous to the 2000–01 school year because MPCP significantly expanded in the 1998–99 school year to include religious schools.[3] The program grew from 1,500 students in 1997–98 to more than 6,000 students in 1998–99 to nearly 8,000 in 1999–2000. During that same time about 70 additional schools joined the program, bringing the total number of participating schools to 91 in 1999–2000.

Measuring Competing Hypotheses

The teacher survey was designed to measure several types of change that may be affected by voucher competition. Each type of change is a dependent variable and is measured by more than one survey question. How each dependent variable might be expected to change depends on one's views of school choice. We designed our survey to evaluate competing hypotheses of the effect of competition on each change variable.

The first dependent variable analyzed was teacher autonomy. We defined teacher autonomy as self-direction over classroom activities and responsibilities. Prominent school choice advocates argue that choice is needed because successful private and charter schools allow their teachers more autonomy than traditional public schools; Chubb and Moe (1990) go so far as to say that teacher and administrator autonomy is the most important influence on student achievement. Beirlein (1996) suggests that public schools may even be subject to a threat of losing teachers to choice schools—charter school teachers report choosing to work in charter schools for such reasons as more freedom and flexibility, increased decision making, dedicated staff, and enhanced accountability. One hypothesis, therefore, is that when faced with competition from private and charter schools, traditional public schools should feel a need to increase their teachers' autonomy or they will risk losing students (and teachers) to schools offering more flexible and creative classrooms (Chubb and Moe 1990).

The opposing hypothesis is that perhaps, as competitive pressures build, public school administrators will be less likely to feel they have the freedom to allow teachers more self-direction in the classroom, because they need to unite teachers as they steer their schools through the marketplace (Teske et al. 2000). Competition may therefore constrain teacher autonomy rather than encourage it. To test these two opposing hypotheses we asked teachers whether any change had occurred in the degree of their autonomy in the past two school years. We asked about six aspects of teacher autonomy and averaged the responses to develop a teacher autonomy index variable.[4]

Teacher empowerment was the second variable analyzed. Teacher empowerment is similar to teacher autonomy but encompasses duties beyond the classroom. In short, it is the notion of a school being run by the teachers themselves, who participate in all decision making directed toward carrying out the school's mission (Bonotti et al. 1999). The greater opportunity for involvement in schoolwide decision making a teacher has, the more empowered that teacher is. The charter school movement in particular is based on this notion of teacher empowerment, which is thought to improve a school in two ways: (1) by improving the performance of teachers and therefore of students, and (2) by reducing the number of entrepreneurial-minded teachers who might leave a school to start their own schools or join the staff of a choice or charter school (Hess et al. 2000).

One hypothesis is that when facing successful, competitive charter or choice schools, public schools will respond by empowering their teachers (Hess et al. 2000). The counterhypothesis is that a public school administrator may feel a need to gain more control over his or her school when entering a competitive market and may not wish to share power with the school's teachers. Therefore, we asked several questions about changes in the teachers' opportunities for involvement in schoolwide decision making in order to test these contradictory theories. Our teacher empowerment variable equaled the average responses to these four questions about schoolwide decision making.[5]

Our third dependent variable encompassed what is probably the most common argument in favor of school choice—that competition will require public schools to become more responsive to parents. Choice and charter advocates contend that in order to maintain enrollment, public schools will find themselves trying harder to satisfy the parents of their students, or, in other words, their consumers, while also trying to attract new parent-consumers (Greene et al. 1999).

But there is an opposing view that schools will have difficulty treating parents as consumers when, in an education marketplace, students are the commodities. In other words, while schools will need to attract as many parents as possible, not all students are desirable. A school will not be deemed successful if it draws only poorly performing students, no matter how many it is able to attract (Ball et al. 1994). Such a school may become less responsive to its parents. To find out whether the responsiveness of MPS teachers to parents had changed in the past two years, we asked questions about the frequency of teachers' interactions with parents. We asked only about interactions in general, intending to include both positive and negative ones. The consumer responsiveness variable equaled the average responses to two questions.[6]

School collaboration was the fourth dependent variable studied. The choice movement, particularly the charter school movement, is partially based on a notion that choice and charter schools will serve as centers of innovation, incubating new methods that, if successful, traditional public schools can adopt to improve their performance (Teske et al. 2000). But opponents of the choice movement point out that this theory assumes communication and collaboration between competing schools and relies on the unlikely notion that schools that view each other as competitors will be willing to share and learn from each other. We measured changes in collaboration by asking teachers about the frequency of their interactions with the staffs of other public and private schools. Our school collaboration variable equaled the average responses to four questions.[7]

If competition does indeed have an effect on public schools by requiring them to respond to market pressures, then certain market-oriented changes in our fifth dependant variable, school climate, would be expected. These changes may involve instruments traditionally seen in the business sphere and not the education sphere, for example, marketing plans and customer surveys. Choice advocates hypothesize that these changes help make schools more aggressively responsive to parents' needs (Greene et al. 1999). Opponents argue that these types of changes will dilute the egalitarian nature of public schooling and result in schools shifting focus from serving the public's interest to serving their own interests (Ball et al. 1994). To measure changes in school climate we asked teachers whether their schools had made any of several specific schoolwide changes over the past two years. The school climate variable equaled the average responses to four questions about schoolwide changes.[8]

Finally, we included two measures of the hypothesis we call direct competitive impacts. The first was our sixth dependent variable, called teachers' awareness of competition, which we measured by asking whether the staff at the teacher's school has discussed the potential impacts of competition.[9] Finally, the seventh dependent variable was itself called direct competitive effects and indicates whether the teacher's school has made changes to retain or attract students in the past two years.[10] We included these two dichotomous measures of direct competitive effects in an attempt to provide a simple gauge of teachers' perceptions of how competition affects their work lives. Measures of teacher autonomy, teacher empowerment, school collaboration, school climate, and consumer responsiveness provided multifaceted measurement of change in teachers' work lives. Including straightforward yes or no measures of direct competitive effects allowed us to broadly assess teachers' perceptions of competition.

Do Teachers Report Change?

Table 3.2 reports the frequency distribution to the questions measuring teachers' perception of change in teacher autonomy, teacher empowerment, and consumer responsiveness. Table 3.3 reports the distribution of responses for the school collaboration, school climate, staff awareness, and direct competitive effects questions. Since some teachers responded "don't know" or did not answer, we also include the number of responses for each variable as well as report the Cronbach's alpha, which quantifies how reliably each grouping of questions measures the same concept.

We find most MPS teachers felt that their level of classroom autonomy has not changed in the past two years. The percentage of teachers responding that their autonomy levels had remained the same ranged between 39 percent for autonomy in teaching methods to 59 percent for autonomy in discipline techniques. The remainder of the teachers' responses were split on whether their autonomy had increased or decreased. This descriptive look at changes in autonomy suggests little support for either the hypothesis that teachers will be given the ability to increase their autonomy or the hypothesis that schools will feel the need to unite by decreasing teachers' level of self-direction.[11]

Our survey results show some evidence of change in teacher empowerment today in MPS compared with two years ago. We find between 42 and 51 percent of MPS teachers indicated they had more opportunity to be involved in decision making in the areas of developing schoolwide policy, hiring other teachers, and marketing their schools to parents of prospective students. In addition, we find evidence that teachers had greater opportunity for involvement in designing the content

Table 3.2. Distribution of Responses: Teacher Autonomy, Teacher Empowerment, and Consumer Responsiveness

	Percent Responding		

Teacher autonomy: In the past two school years or so, have you experienced more or less autonomy than before in each of the following areas?

	More	Same	Less
Use of outside classroom resources	32	49	14
Teaching methods you use	37	39	20
Daily time management	25	40	32
Yearly scheduling	17	45	35
Classroom curriculum	25	41	31
Discipline techniques	25	59	13
N			419
Cronbach's Alpha			0.86

Teacher empowerment: In the past two school years or so, have you experienced more or less opportunity for involvement than before in each of the following areas?

	More	Same	Less
Developing schoolwide policy	42	35	20
Hiring other teachers	51	28	14
Designing professional development opportunities	37	42	16
Marketing the school	48	37	10
N			412
Cronbach's Alpha			0.77

Consumer responsiveness: Please indicate whether the amount of time you spend each school year doing each of the following increased, decreased, or stayed about the same in the past two school years or so:

	Increased	Same	Decreased
Responding to parents' concerns	44	47	6
Seeking input from parents	42	49	6
N			412
Cronbach's Alpha			0.93

Table 3.3. Distribution of Responses: Collaboration, School Climate, Awareness of Competition, and Direct Competitive Impacts

	Percent Responding

Collaboration: Do you strongly agree, agree, disagree, or strongly disagree with each of the following statements: In the past two school years or so I have . . .

	Agree	Disagree
Become more knowledgeable about the educational practices of nearby MPS schools	41	54
Become more knowledgeable about the educational practices of nearby private schools	23	74
Interacted more often on a professional level with teachers or administrators from private schools	12	85
Interacted more often on a professional level with teachers or administrators from charter schools	12	86
N		444
Cronbach's Alpha		0.85

School Climate: In the past two school years or so, has your school done any of the following?

	Yes	No	Don't Know
Created a new school logo	21	72	4
Established new partnerships with outside organizations	61	24	12
Opened before- or after-school programs	73	21	3
Offered new curricular course(s)	55	32	9
Begun distributing school information door-to-door	21	47	29
Hosted additional open houses for potential students	50	41	7
Created a new school marketing plan	34	39	25
Created a new school website	52	33	12
Developed a new school mission	37	50	10
N			322
Cronbach's Alpha			0.68

Awareness: Please indicate whether, in your opinion, the following is true or false:

	True	False	Don't Know
The staff at your school discusses the possible impacts of competition on your enrollment	77	14	7
N			386

Direct Impacts: Has your school, in the past two school years or so:

	Yes	No	Did Not Answer
Made any changes to retain or attract students?	67	22	11
N			376

of their professional development days (37 percent). The descriptive analysis suggests some degree of support for the hypothesis that schools will respond to competition by empowering their teachers.

As for consumer responsiveness, we find more teachers reported that their interactions with parents remained the same over the past two school years, but a large number believed they had interacted more often with parents. Very few, just 6 percent on each question, felt their communications with parents had decreased in that time period. These results suggest support for the idea that, in light of competition, teachers become more, not less, responsive to consumers.

Our respondents indicated that collaboration among schools, including other MPS schools, had not increased over the past two years. Teachers at all grade levels told us they are not more knowledgeable about the educational practices of nearby schools (54 percent), especially private schools (74 percent), now than they were two years ago. Nor did MPS teachers feel their amount of interaction with individual teachers from non-MPS schools had increased; it makes little difference whether the other teachers were from private (85 percent) or charter schools (86 percent). Overall, the data suggest that in the first two years of expanded choice, public school teachers did not perceive school collaboration to have increased.

Many teachers indicated that their schools have experienced changes in school climate. This suggests that competition may be resulting in specific changes within the school. Although these changes may be responses to increased competition, the most frequent changes are not obviously promotional techniques. For example, the three most frequently mentioned changes were educational enhancements— before/after school programs (73 percent), new partnerships with businesses or community organizations (61 percent), and new courses (55 percent)—while marketing plans (34 percent), new logos (21 percent), and door-to-door literature distribution (21 percent) have not been widely implemented. A substantial number of teachers do not know whether their schools have made any of these changes, which means teachers may be underreporting the use of these techniques.

When it comes to direct competitive effects as measured by staff discussions of competition and changes to retain or attract students, we find that over three-fourths of teachers at all grade levels said their school staffs have discussed the possible impacts of competition on enrollment. In order to find all possible changes that could have been spurred by competition or teacher discussions about competition, we concluded the survey by asking simply, "Has your school, in the last two school years or so, made any changes to retain or attract students." Overall, two-thirds of the teachers indicated that, yes, their school has made such changes.

When asked for examples of the types of changes to retain or attract students that were made or are anticipated, teachers gave a wide variety of examples. These responses are coded into three separate categories in table 3.4: marketing/publicity, schoolwide reform/changes, and creation of special programs. Most of the responses fall within the more academically oriented categories of schoolwide reform and special programs rather than within the realm of marketing.

The findings reported above illustrate a great deal of variation in the number of teachers who reported changes over the past two years in teacher autonomy, teacher empowerment, consumer responsiveness, and school climate. In addition, teachers did not feel there has been an increase in the amount of collaboration with other schools. Yet a majority of teachers discussed the potential impacts of competition with their colleagues. Most teachers also felt that their school had made changes in the past two years to retain or attract students. On the whole it appears that, at a minimum, teaching staffs have discussed the potential impacts of competition and made some changes in response. When it comes to the types of schoolwide changes made, however, no clear patterns are evident.

Table 3.4. Distribution of Responses: Changes Made to Retain or Attract Students

	Responses (N)	Percent of Total Responses
Schoolwide Reforms/Changes		
Curricular changes/new school focus	38	5.60
K4/All-day K5	30	4.50
Added technology resources or instruction	27	4.00
Special Programs		
Before- and after-school care	77	11.40
Other specific special programs	35	5.20
Partnerships/mentoring/tutoring	30	4.50
Marketing/Publicity		
Open houses/orientation sessions	40	5.90
Direct recruitment of students or families	28	4.20
Marketing/publicity, in general	26	3.90

Are the Changes the Result of Competition?

Knowing now that teachers have reported some changes in their work lives during two years of tremendous growth in school choice, we are left with the question of whether these changes resulted from competition with voucher schools. To analyze this we begin by describing our independent variables.

The independent variable of interest, labeled competitive presence, was the variable we hypothesized would affect our dependent variables. Competitive presence may be real or potential, that is, there may or may not be a competing voucher school in operation. But we expect schools to respond to either type of presence because a school in Milwaukee operates in a competitive environment regardless of whether there are competing schools nearby (Hess et al. 2000). We chose to measure competitive presence by counting the number of private voucher schools offering similar grade levels within a half-mile radius of the public school, believing that if any competitive effects from vouchers are to be found, they would most likely be at the school building level (Geller et al. 2000). We used geographic mapping software to determine the number and enrollment of private schools participating in MPCP within a half-mile radius of each public school represented by a survey respondent. Competitive presence equaled zero if no similar voucher schools were nearby, and one if at least one similar voucher school was within a half mile.[12] We called a zero value potential competitive threat, as no competing schools were nearby, while a one value was a real or existent competitive presence.

In order to ensure that we measured only the effects of competitive presence on our dependent variables and not the effects of some other factor, we controlled for the following factors:

- Experience of teacher: More experienced teachers may be less inclined to report change over the last two years than less experienced teachers, who are experiencing many things for the first time. Our measure of experience is the total number of years the teacher has taught in MPS and ranged from seven to thirty-seven years.[13]
- Support for private school choice: Public school teacher unions are traditionally unsupportive of private school choice, which may result in public school teachers opposing school choice (Grammatico 2001). In our sample, 73 percent of teachers did not support private school choice. Because support for choice may affect how teachers view changes that occur within their school, we included a variable that equaled one if the teacher supported choice, or zero otherwise.
- School characteristics: The surroundings in which the teacher works can affect changes experienced by the teacher; for this reason, we controlled for several school-level factors.

These included teacher stability, defined as the average percent of staff that returned to the school in 1998–99 and 1999–2000;[14] administrative tenure, measured as the number of years the principal has been at the school; and grade level.[15] We included grade level because MPCP schools have many more options available for elementary and middle school students than for high school students; therefore, we expected elementary and middle school teachers to be more sensitive to the effects of competition than high school teachers.[16]

- Change in enrollment: Some researchers anticipate that public schools experiencing declining enrollments may be more likely to initiate change (Ball et al. 1994). In addition, because MPS schools are funded on a per-pupil basis, enrollment differences will also reflect resource differences. We measured enrollment change as the percent change in the total number of full-time students from 1997–98 to 1999–2000. We expected that schools experiencing enrollment loss were more likely to make changes.

- Other school reform: Like most large, urban school districts, MPS has multiple ongoing reforms at any one point in time and introduced many reform initiatives during the tremendous growth in choice enrollment between 1998 and 2000 in particular. Perhaps the most significant of these district-led reforms is decentralization, which shifts much of the district's budgeting and management duties from the central office to the schools, thereby increasing the responsibilities of school staff at the building level. However, effects on schools due to district-led policy changes such as decentralization would be more likely to occur uniformly across all schools in the district than would competitive effects, which are more likely to be influenced by geography or other factors (Hess et al. 2000). Therefore, we did not control for decentralization. Another reform that began in MPS during the last two years, however, called the Neighborhood Schools Initiative (NSI), does affect schools differently. NSI is a plan to reduce busing in MPS by encouraging students to attend their neighborhood schools; NSI may therefore be characterized as the antithesis of choice. We controlled for change that might be caused by NSI rather than by competition by including a variable that equaled one if a school was a targeted school under NSI, or zero otherwise. We anticipated that schools targeted for NSI implementation will experience greater change.

For an initial analysis of whether there is any relation between the competitive presence of nearby voucher schools and changes in MPS teachers' work lives, we performed a difference of means test. This test affords a simple look at the relationship between our independent variable, competitive presence, and each of our seven dependent variables. Table 3.5 shows that for most of our dependent variables, there does not appear to be a relationship between the number of voucher schools nearby[17] and the amount of change in a school as reported by the teachers. Neither teacher autonomy, teacher empowerment, consumer responsiveness, school collaboration, nor staff awareness of competition seems to be affected by the number of competing voucher schools nearby. Comparing the average change for each of these five variables when there are no choice schools nearby (the competitive threat is merely potential) with the average change when there is at least one choice school within a half-mile (an existent competitive presence) resulted in statistically insignificant differences in all cases. For two of our dependent variables, however, the test results are more interesting. We find teachers were significantly *less* likely to report their schools' climates had changed or their schools had made changes to retain or attract students when there was the competitive presence of at least one voucher school nearby.

Table 3.5. Competitive Effects of Nearby Choice Schools on Teacher Work-Lives

	Number of MPCP Schools within Half-Mile Radius	
	0 Schools "Potential Competitive Threat" Mean	1 to 5 Schools "Existent Competitive Presence" Mean
Teacher autonomy: In the past two school years or so, have you experienced more or less autonomy than before in each of the following areas (on a scale from 1 to 5 with 5 equal to much less)?	2.95 (N = 181)	3.03 (N = 219)
Teacher empowerment: In the past two school years or so, have you experienced more or less opportunity for involvement than before in each of the following areas (on a scale from 1 to 5 with 5 equal to much less)?	2.69 (N = 175)	2.62 (N = 217)
Consumer responsiveness: Please indicate whether the amount of time you spend each school year responding to parents' concerns and seeking input from parents increased, decreased, or stayed about the same in the past two school years or so (1 equals increased, 2 stayed the same, 3 decreased).	1.41 (N = 189)	1.38 (N = 233)
Collaboration: Do you agree or disagree in the past two school years or so you have become more knowledgeable about or interacted with other schools (1 = strongly agree with 4 equal to strongly disagree)?	2.91 (N = 191)	2.98 (N = 233)
Awareness: Please indicate whether, in your opinion, the following is true or false: staff at your school discusses the possible impacts of competition on your enrollment (1 = true, 2 = false).	1.19 (N = 179)	1.12 (N = 217)
School climate: In the past two years or so, has your school done any of the following, school-wide changes (1 = yes, 2 = no)?	1.21 (N = 193)	1.35 (N = 234)*
Direct impacts: Has your school, in the past two school years or so, made any changes to retain or attract students (1 = yes, 2 = no)?	1.16 (N = 175)	1.33 (N = 211)*

* $p < .05$

The results of this initial analysis are quite surprising. Direct competition from private voucher schools is not related to teacher-reported changes in teacher empowerment, teacher autonomy, consumer responsiveness, school collaboration, or staff awareness of competition. Therefore, except for changes in school climate and the changes teachers say have been made by their schools to retain or attract students, it does not appear that competition has an effect on our dependent variables. And for the two variables that do appear affected, the relationship is the opposite of what would be expected. From the results of this simple test, it appears that none of our various hypotheses prove true—competition from nearby voucher schools does not lead public schools to make changes.

Because of the interesting results for the school climate and direct competitive effects variables, we further explored a potential causal relationship using OLS regression. The relationships found in our difference of means test largely continued when we ran the full analysis. The results presented in table 3.6 indicate that for three dependent variables, teacher autonomy, teacher empowerment, and consumer responsiveness, the competitive presence of nearby voucher schools cannot explain the variance. We therefore find no support for a relationship between competition and change in teacher work lives as measured by these three variables.[18]

Our model is statistically significant, however, for explaining a small fraction of the variance in school collaboration, teacher-reported changes in school climate, teachers' discussions of competition, and schools' changes to retain or attract students. Competitive presence and the change in teachers' discussions of potential competitive effects appear to be positively related, meaning the more nearby voucher competition a public school has, the more its teachers discuss competitive effects. But this relationship is not statistically significant. Competitive presence and changes in school climate and school collaboration appear negatively related, though insignificant.

Given that nearby voucher competition does not explain these changes, what other factors could have an influence on changes in teachers' discussions about competitive effects, school collaboration, and changes in school climate? As depicted in table 3.6, we find that, although it is not statistically significant, teacher stability, grade level of the school, administrative tenure, enrollment change, and the teachers' support for choice have some explanatory power. For instance, the more turnover in the teaching staff at a school, the more likely the staff was to discuss the potential impacts of competition. In addition, teaching staffs at upper grade levels, primarily high school, were less likely to have discussions about competitive effects than lower grade level teachers. Moreover, teachers who support choice were less likely to report that the staff of their school is discussing the possible impacts of competition than were teachers who did not support choice. Increases in teacher collaboration are positively related to being a targeted school under Milwaukee's NSI. Finally, contrary to our expectations, teachers in schools experiencing increases in enrollment were more likely to report changes in school climate than those in schools experiencing declining enrollment.

Table 3.6 also confirms our findings from the difference of means test that competitive presence is significantly related to schools making changes to retain or attract students. Again, this relationship is not in the hypothesized direction—teachers in MPS schools that have competing voucher schools located nearby were significantly *less* likely to report their schools had made changes to retain or attract students than those in schools without a nearby competitive presence. In addition, none of our control variables are significantly related to teacher-reported changes to retain or attract students.

Does this mean that the changes schools made to retain or attract students were somehow not made in response to competition? Our results seem to support this conclusion. Yet we note that just because the schools in which teachers reported changes were not the same

Table 3.6. Unstandardized OLS Regression Coefficients for Competitive Effects on Teacher Work Lives

Independent Variables	Model 1 Teacher Autonomy (Larger number indicates increase in autonomy)	Model 2 Teacher Empowerment (Larger number indicates increase in empowerment)	Model 3 Consumer Responsiveness (Larger number indicates increased responsiveness)	Model 4 Teacher Collaboration (Larger number indicates increasing collaboration)	Model 5 Changes in School Climate (Larger number indicates improved climate)	Model 6 Discussion of Competition (Larger number indicates discussing competition)	Model 7 Changes to Retain or Attract Students (Larger number indicates making changes)
School Level Variables							
Competitive threat	0.06 (0.09)	−0.05 (0.06)	−0.08 (0.06)	−0.1 (.06)	−0.04 (.04)	0.06 (0.04)	−0.14 (0.05)**
Enrollment change	−0.64 (0.65)	0.47 (0.43)	0.52 (0.42)	−0.31 (.43)	0.48 (0.27)*	−0.24 (0.29)	−0.05 (0.36)
Teacher stability	−0.01 (0.006)*	0.003 (0.004)	−0.0002 (0.004)	0.001 (.004)	0.0001 (0.002)	−0.01 (0.002)**	−0.002 (0.003)

	(1)	(2)	(3)	(4)	(5)	(6)	(7)
Administrative tenure	0.009	−0.004	0.0002	0.02	−0.014	−0.01	0.006
	(0.01)	(0.006)	(0.006)	(.006)**	(0.004)**	(0.004)	(0.005)
Grade level	−0.01	−0.05	−0.04	−0.005	0.01	0.08	−0.02
	(0.04)	(0.03)**	(0.03)	(.03)	(.02)	(0.02)**	(0.02)
Neighborhood school initiative	0.08	0.09	0.05	0.24	0.08	−0.07	0.08
	(0.13)	(0.09)	(0.09)	(.09)**	(.05)	(0.06)	(0.08)
Individual Level Variables							
Teacher experience	0.003	0.001	0.002	−0.002	0.003	−0.001	−0.004
	(0.006)	(0.004)	(0.004)	(.004)	(.002)	(0.002)	(0.003)
Teacher support for choice	−0.06	−0.03	−0.1	0.11	0.03	0.08	0.03
	(0.1)	(0.06)	(0.06)	(.06)*	(.04)	(0.04)*	(0.05)
Intercept	3.77	0.238	1.5	−3.13	−1.32	−0.52	−0.62
(F-test) p < .001	NS	NS	NS	NS	3.43	4.76	3.06
Adjusted R^2	0.02	0.02	0.02	0.03	0.06	0.07	0.04
N	389	382	412	444	322	386	376
	Model Insignificant	*Model Insignificant*	*Model Insignificant*	*Model Insignificant*	*Model Significant*	*Model Significant*	*Model Significant*

*p < .10; **p < .05 (two-tailed)

Note: Standard errors are in parentheses.

schools experiencing an existent competitive presence from nearby voucher schools does not necessarily mean that competition has not caused these changes. One explanation could be that voucher schools purposefully locate near public schools known to be less innovative, seeing them as less competitive, although this seems unlikely. Another explanation is that public schools surrounded by long-established private schools no longer consider them competition but have instead found ways to exist in equilibrium. Or perhaps public schools find that once actual competition is established, they are able to compete without making changes—the potential threat of voucher competition does more to induce change in a public school than does the actual competition. Further research is needed to determine whether any of these explanations are true.

Competition and Public School Performance

For parents' actions in choosing private schools to lead to accountability for public schools, there must be a systematic relationship between actual competition and changes in public schools. According to our teacher survey, there is no such relationship. Since teacher-reported changes do not provide evidence that competitive presence causes a response in public schools, we sought evidence elsewhere. We now go beyond our teacher survey and ask, Does nearby voucher competition induce changes in public school quality?

We measured school quality by standardized achievement test scores of MPS schools. To put our discussion of achievement scores in context, we compare in figure 3.1 the average MPS test scores with the statewide average test scores. The tests used are the fourth and eighth grade Wisconsin Knowledge and Concepts Exams (WKCE). The scores are the combined average national percentile rank for reading and math. The national percentile rank compares the aggregated district score with

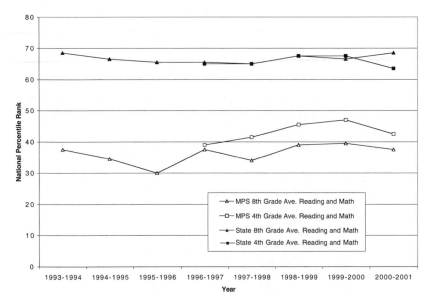

Figure 3.1. Wisconsin Knowledge and Concepts Exam National Percentile Ranks: Combined Average Reading and Math for Milwaukee Public Schools and State, 1993–94 to 2000–01

the scores of other students from districts across the nation who are at the same grade level and took the test at a comparable time of year. The higher the percentile rank, the better the district has scored compared to the national group. The WKCE was mandated for eighth grade in the 1993–94 school year and for fourth grade in 1996–97.

The voucher program has been in existence since 1990–91; as noted, however, it remained a small program until the 1998–99 school year. Thus, if voucher competition is related to overall school performance, we should expect to see competitive gains in MPS scores as early as the 1997–98 school year. In fact, as figure 3.1 shows, no such gains have occurred. Combined math and reading scores remained unchanged in eighth grade from 1998–99 to 1999–2000 and decreased in 2000–01.

Fourth grade combined math and reading scores increased slightly from 1998–99 to 1999–2000 but decreased four and a half percentage points in 2000–01.

Therefore, no competition-induced effects are apparent for MPS as a whole. Yet, as the adage goes, reforming a school district is like trying to turn an ocean liner around; individual schools should be more responsive. We are more likely to see competitive effects at the individual school building level. For every elementary, middle, and K–8 MPS school, we examined school scores on statewide standardized tests between 1997–98 and 1999–2000.[19] We analyzed the percentage of students in a school scoring at a level of proficient or above on the fourth and/or eighth grade WKCE in reading and math. To determine whether competition influences public schools to improve, we calculated both the average math and reading scores over the three-year period and the change in math and reading scores.

As shown in table 3.7, we find no significant correlation between school performance and voucher competition, again, as measured by the competitive presence of nearby voucher schools.[20] Across all four achievement measures there is no significant relationship between performance of MPS schools and the presence of nearby voucher schools. In fact, for reading scores, the relationship is not even in the direction market theory would predict. For public schools with no voucher schools within a half mile, the average three-year increase from 1997–98 to 1999–2000 in the percent of students scoring proficient or above in reading was twice that of schools with at least one voucher school nearby.

For math scores, on the other hand, the relationship to competition is in the predicted direction, although it is insignificant. The three-year average change in math scores from 1997–98 to 1999–2000 for schools within the competitive presence of nearby voucher schools was higher than for schools without any voucher schools nearby.[21]

The story of two MPS schools further illustrates how competi-

Table 3.7. Competitive Effects of Nearby Choice Schools on Public School Performance, 1997–98 to 1999–2000

National Percentile Rankings: Wisconsin 4th and 8th Grade Knowledge and Concepts Exams	Number of MPCP Schools within Half-Mile Radius	
	0 Schools "Potential Competitive Threat" Mean	1 to 5 Schools "Existent Competitive Presence" Mean
Three-year average reading score	43.61	41.93
Three-year average math score	32.97	35.54
Three-year change in reading scores	8.16	4.82
Three-year change in math scores	23.16	25.43

tion does not appear to be related to improvements in public school performance. For example, Twenty-seventh Street School had one of the greatest increases in reading scores over this three-year period; its fourth grade reading proficiency increased by 34 percentage points. There were two voucher schools within a half mile of Twenty-seventh Street School enrolling a total of 604 voucher students. In contrast, one of the schools experiencing the greatest decline in reading proficiency scores was Westside Academy, only a short distance from Twenty-seventh Street School. Fourth grade reading proficiency at Westside Academy declined by 25 percentage points during the time period under study. Yet the nearby voucher competition was similar to that of neighboring Twenty-seventh Street School, with two voucher schools within a half mile enrolling a total of 304 voucher students. In the case of these two public schools, similar competition did not lead to similar changes in performance. Even more interesting is that despite Twenty-seventh Street School's competitiveness, as evidenced by its strong gains in reading, it was closed down by MPS in the 2001–02 school year because of facility needs. The school's seeming success in the face of competition was not enough to keep it open.

Our results indicate that the competitive presence of nearby voucher schools appears to have no discernable impact on individual public school performance. And while these results are surprising, they are not unique; researchers in Georgia have reported similar findings on a districtwide analysis (Geller et al. 2001).[22] There may be competition-related explanations for this outcome. For example, voucher schools may choose to locate near low-performing public schools, or voucher schools may lure high-performing students away from public schools. Even if some such phenomenon is at work, the theory that a competitive education marketplace will improve public school performance has not proven accurate. In Milwaukee, voucher competition does not result in increased achievement of public schools.

What Our Findings Mean for Accountability

In the end, our ability to predict changes or improvements in public schools on the basis of the existence of nearby voucher competition is very limited. Over the past two school years, despite a 400 percent increase in enrollment in Milwaukee's private school voucher program, MPS teachers report little change in teacher autonomy, school collaboration, or responsiveness to parents. And in the areas in which teachers do report change—teacher empowerment and staff awareness of competition—the changes appear unrelated to the competitive presence of nearby voucher schools. In fact, where a relationship is found, that is, in the case of school climate, there is evidence that a public school may be *less* likely to make changes when there are voucher schools nearby. Most interesting, a school with voucher schools nearby is *significantly less* likely to make changes to retain or attract students—exactly the opposite of what would be expected of a school facing imminent competition. Finally, a separate analysis indicates that the presence of nearby voucher schools has no effect on a school's change in reading or math achievement over the past three years.

Therefore, merely counting the number of voucher schools in proximity to a Milwaukee public school provides very little information about that school's response to competition by the voucher program. In fact, because we find public schools that are not located near any voucher schools to be the ones more likely to make changes, it seems that the general atmosphere of competition throughout the city may be the more effective change agent.

Even so, we find once more that the evidence in Milwaukee does not support the arguments for school choice. Again, an important link to accountability is missing—parents' actions are not provoking competitive response by public schools. In chapter 2 we illustrated how private schools are failing to respond to parents' choices. Public schools' responses to competition, whether general or proximate, are similarly lackluster. The result is that in Milwaukee, neither voucher nor public school parents appear to be receiving the promised educational benefits of competition through school choice.

CHAPTER FOUR

What Parents Know

An Examination of Informed Consumers

U ntil now we have been focusing on accountability by probing the responsiveness of both voucher and public schools to parents. In each case we have found this response to be deficient. We turn our attention in chapters 4 and 5 toward understanding whether parents are able to send a clear message to schools by the act of choosing a school. We examine first the existence of informed consumers.

In traditional, assignment-based public school systems school choice proponents believe parents have little incentive to gather information about schools because they do not select the schools their children attend; educators and elected school boards control school assignment. School choice proponents hope school choice will eliminate these impediments to parental control over education. The belief is that the empowering of parents to choose where their children attend school also allows parents to learn more about and actively participate in schools.[1]

School choice can take many forms and may therefore differ in the degree to which it induces parents to gather information. For instance, tuition-paying parents selecting private schools make up the largest competitive education market in the country. At the other extreme are public school district students, who are assigned to schools solely on the basis of their residency. Some public school districts allow parents limited choices, which can include specialty or magnet schools. Other public school districts give first preference to neighborhood students and then open the remaining seats to students from across the district. Finally, a few public school districts have open enrollment throughout the district, in which parents are able to select across all available options and a lottery is held for seat assignment.

Despite the fact that school choice exists widely in private education and to some degree in various public school districts, we know little about the incentives these different choice systems provide parents when gathering schooling information. We would hypothesize that the more open the market, the more likely parents are to act as true consumers. That is, the fewer restrictions on a parent's ability to choose, the more likely the parent is to make a rational, beneficial decision. By rational and beneficial we mean a decision that satisfies the varying needs of parents in selecting a school. To make such a decision, however, parents need information. The debate over accountability is undeniably linked with the adequacy of information parents have about schools. To test our hypothesis, in this chapter we examine across various types of choice systems the amount of information parent consumers have about the schools they select, and whether these parents send consistent signals when choosing.

Accountability and School Choice

Research suggests that if parents' choices are to serve as an adequate school accountability system, they need to be based on high levels of information. Yet even Chubb and Moe acknowledge that markets are inevitably subject to all sorts of real-world imperfections, and one of these is that consumers may be too poorly informed to make choices that are truly in their best interests (1990: 34). Others point out that individuals having lower incomes and less education are less likely to possess adequate information (Henig 1999: 74). In addition, survey research has demonstrated that parents are rather uninformed about their education choices, and many are unaware of choice programs that exist for their children (Public Agenda 1999).

Within these real-world limitations, Schneider and his coauthors studied parent-consumers of public school choice in four school districts. The major focus of their work was the ways in which school choice altered parents' incentives and in turn affected their behavior (2000). They addressed a number of issues relating to parental behavior, paying particular attention to the argument put forth by choice proponents that school choice increases the incentives for parents to obtain information about the schools their children attend. They found overall that most parents are uninformed about their schools; however, they found a subset of parents who are informed consumers. In their study, these informed consumers are more likely to be parents who actively chose their children's schools rather than having the district assign them a school. They identify these active, informed parents as marginal consumers. They argue that the marginal consumer, by making the best choices for him or herself, can strengthen overall parental accountability in two ways. First, marginal educational consumers influence other consumers by their market behavior, even without directly communicating with the less-informed parents. Second, marginal consumers pressure schools to improve. Therefore, for the education market to function effectively, only a subset of parents needs to be well informed about the various educational options their schools offer (Schneider et al. 1998: 784; for a more detailed discussion, see Schneider et al. 2000).

Other research on parental decision making suggests that parents who choose do not always send clear signals about their decisions to leave one school for another. Manna examined data from parent surveys conducted from 1990-91 to 1994–95 as part of an evaluation of the MPCP. In exploring these questions, Manna described the possible interplay between the decisions parents made in choosing or leaving a school and the inferences school officials (and other parents) might draw from them. The author concluded that the messages parents send by their decisions to leave the public schools are not always clear (Manna 1999). Manna's research questions whether such choosers really influence other consumers or pressure schools to improve. Neither of the above studies directly examines school choice accountability, yet because of their focus on parent-consumers, their findings have implications for how schools participating in a choice system are held accountable.

Research Design

The research design we use borrows from the above analyses of choice by Schneider et al. (2000), Manna (1999), and also Witte (1991–95).[2] We used data from long-established Milwaukee choice programs other than vouchers because data on participating voucher parents are not available to the public and because most growth in the Milwaukee voucher program occurred within the last few years. Our aim was to identify informed consumers who send consistent signals.[3] If an efficiently operating market system of accountability, in the form of informed consumers, can exist, evidence of it is more likely in choice programs that are well established. Finding such evidence would support placing the responsibility for accountability in the hands of parents.

We surveyed parents who chose their schools in Milwaukee and the surrounding suburbs under various choice systems. As noted in chapter 1, Milwaukee parents can select among a number of choice programs for their children. For this study we examined the following educational options for parents in the Milwaukee area: both aspects of the interdistrict Chapter 220 program (that is, suburban students choosing city schools as well as city students choosing suburban schools); the intradistrict three-choice selection process within MPS; and traditional tuition-based private schooling.

Chapter 220 Interdistrict Public School Choice

The Chapter 220 program, the oldest of Milwaukee's parental option programs, was established in 1976 to promote racial integration of Milwaukee and its surrounding suburban districts. The implementation of the program coincided with a federal court order for desegregation in Milwaukee, the result of declining nonminority enrollment in the city. It is a targeted choice program because only a minority pupil residing in a district with a concentration of minority pupils of 30 percent or greater may transfer into an adjacent district with 30 percent or less minority pupils. Likewise, majority students residing in districts with low numbers of minority students may transfer into an adjacent district with the higher specified concentrations.[4] In the case of minority students each applicant can list up to three suburban districts but *cannot* choose specific schools within these districts. MPS conducts a random selection process to pick students and match them with their chosen districts, where they are assigned a school. If a student is not accepted at a preferred suburban district, the student is placed on a waiting list, from which he or she may be admitted until mid-December. A student must reapply for the program the following year if he or she is not selected off the waiting list. In our analysis we refer to this group of parents as Milwaukee 220. Suburban parents applying to MPS can apply to any of the more than 150 schools. We identify this group of parents as Suburban 220.

Intradistrict Public School Choice

The intradistrict public school choice system is made up of parents in MPS who chose to send their children to either a citywide specialty or regular school. Unlike parents in many public school systems, MPS parents must participate in a three-choice selection process implemented in 1991–92 when enrolling their children. Therefore, only a small percentage of parents whose children currently attend MPS did not choose the schools their children attend. The MPS three-choice selection process is not a "controlled choice" process, as that term is used by other cities in the nation. Although Milwaukee's elementary students are limited to choosing among schools in particular areas of the city—areas that are drawn to be as racially balanced as possible—a student's choice of a particular school is, for the most part, not restricted by racial parameters. There are some exceptions to this general rule, however, and waiting lists for the citywide specialty schools are maintained by race. In addition, the school board has a policy of ensuring that any child who desires a racially balanced school has the opportunity to attend one. According to an April 1999 report on school selection in MPS, of the 20,109 students indicating their top three school choices for 1999–2000, 16,512, or 82 percent, were accepted to their first choice school. Another 1,329 students were accepted to their second or third choice school. Our intradistrict choice system is divided into two different categories depending on whether a parent selected a citywide or a regular MPS school.

Tuition-Based Private School Choice

The final choice system that is under study involves parents who send their children to private schools.[5] Approximately 20,000 students who reside in Milwaukee attend private school. Traditional tuition-based private school choice is not a targeted program; parents must have the financial ability to pay for tuition.

As table 4.1 illustrates, 144,381 Milwaukee area students participate in these choice systems.

Survey Methodology

Do these choice systems provide different incentives to parents to gather information? To answer this we conducted a phone survey in fall 1999 of parents whose children participated in one of the choice

Table 4.1. Schooling Options in the Milwaukee Metropolitan Area

Program	Parent Eligibility	Number of Participating Schools or Districts	Number of Participating Milwaukee Students
Citywide Milwaukee Public Schools*	Milwaukee resident	38 (schools)	20,552
Regular Milwaukee Public Schools*	Milwaukee resident	119 (schools)	76,086
Interdistrict Chapter 220 Program			
Milwaukee minority parents (Milwaukee 220)**	Minority Milwaukee resident	140 (schools)	4,859 (FTE)
Suburban nonminority parents (Suburban 220)**	Nonminority resident of participating suburban district	160 (schools)	588 (FTE)
Charter schools***	Milwaukee resident	11 (schools)	5,048 (FTE)
Statewide open enrollment***	Resident of any Wisconsin public school district	426 (districts)	840
Milwaukee Parental Choice Program***	Low-income Milwaukee resident	103 (schools)	9,200 (FTE)
Traditional tuition-based private school (includes MPCP)**	Determined by independent schools	117 (schools)	27,208

* Data from 1999–2000 school year.
** Data from 1998–99 school year.
*** Data from 2000–01.

Table 4.2. Completed Phone Interviews by Category

Category	Completed Interviews	Percent of Total
Milwaukee 220[1]	201	30
Attend MPS[2]	234	35
Suburban 220[3]	63	9
Attend private school	180	27
Total	678	101

[1] MPS 220 participants are those parents who reside in Milwaukee and participate in the 220 program by sending their children to a participating suburban district.
[2] Includes both MPS citywide and MPS regular.
[3] Suburban 220 participants include parents who reside in a district outside of Milwaukee and sent their children to MPS by participating in the Chapter 220 program.
Note: Total does not add up to 100 percent because of rounding.

programs (table 4.2). The survey included eighty questions and took approximately twenty-one minutes to complete. To reduce the number of total questions asked of any one respondent, fourteen of the eighty questions were asked only of the odd-numbered respondents and another set of fourteen were asked only of even-numbered respondents. This not only ensured that all groups would be equally represented in these questions, but also reduced the overall length of the survey. The survey included eighteen questions recorded for statistical purposes only. These questions allow for an understanding of the characteristics of the survey respondents. In addition, they make it possible to compare respondents by controlling for a number of personal characteristics theoretically related to education decisions.

Survey questions were designed to fit into one or more of four themes: perception of particular schools/programs, accessibility of information, satisfaction with school and the schooling option program, and parental involvement. In this chapter we focus on questions related to accessibility of information.

The survey was conducted as part of a contract with MPS. In designing the survey we borrowed the wording of questions from surveys used by Schneider and his coauthors (2000) and by Witte (1990–

95) in order to allow for replication of the analyses used by these authors and by authors who rely on their data. The majority of questions were designed to assist MPS in learning more about the actions of parents who participated in various choice programs. After it was determined which choice program the family participated in, that parent was asked how many of their children were enrolled in the program.[6] If more than one, the parent was asked to limit his or her answers to the child who was having the next birthday. This ensured a random sample of children in all grade levels.[7] It also ensured that answers were unique to one child. The total number of completed surveys was 678, a response rate of 20 percent.[8]

Table 4.3 illustrates the distribution of sampled respondents on several social characteristics. Parents whose children attend MPS or participate in the Milwaukee 220 program have very similar characteristics in terms of age, marital status and race, but Milwaukee 220 parents are wealthier and more likely to be college educated. Suburban 220 participants are more likely to be college graduates and have the highest income of all surveyed groups.

Findings: A First Look at the Information Level of Parent Consumers

We examined how much knowledge parents have about certain key characteristics of the schools their children attend. We asked half of our survey respondents questions about several school characteristics. The specific wording of the questions is as follows: (1) *What do you think is the percentage of students in [INSERT SCHOOL] who are eligible for free or reduced-price lunch?* Less than 50%, 51%–75%, Greater than 75%. (2) *What do you think is the percentage of students in [INSERT SCHOOL] who have reading scores at or above grade level?* Less than 50%, 51%–75%, Greater than 75%. (3) *We'd like you to think about the racial makeup of [Name of Child] school. In particular we'd like you to tell us*

Table 4.3. Percentage Distribution of Sampled Respondents on Selected Social Characteristics

	Average Age in Years of Respondents	Percent Married	Percent College Graduate or Higher	Percent Nonwhite	Percent Catholic	Percent Indicating Household Income for 1998 was over $40,000
Milwaukee 220	37	57	30	81*	20	40
Attend MPS	39	56	22	70	21	32
Suburban 220	42	86	57	10*	48	67
Attend private school	40	79	35	29	28	50
Total	39	68	33	57	28	54

* The data are on the parent, not the child. In order for a student to participate in the Chapter 220 program they have to represent the minority population in Milwaukee and the majority population in the suburbs. Biracial and transracial families can explain the 19 percent of parents of MPS 220 participants who are white and the 10 percent of Suburban 220 parents who are nonwhite.

what percentage of students in [INSERT SCHOOL] you think are African American? 0–9%, 10%–25%, 26%–50%, 51%–75%, 76%–100%. We used a broad measure of knowledge by allowing the survey respondent to select within a range of percentages of a school's population on all three questions. These variables were included in the survey because we felt they would give us an opportunity to measure accuracy of information for a subset of the population. Schneider et al. (2000) included similar questions in their survey of school choice in four different districts.[9] We compared this selection with the actual data for the child's school.[10] Table 4.4 illustrates by program the accuracy of parental information on these characteristics.

Accuracy is highest for Milwaukee 220 parents on the percentage eligible for free or reduced-price lunch. Accuracy is lowest for MPS citywide parents who are more likely to believe that the percentage eligible for free or reduced-price lunch is lower than actual. On average, half the parents do not possess accurate information on these school characteristics. This is similar to Schneider et al.'s (2000: chap. 7) findings concerning only public school choosers. What is unique about our findings is that they are a direct comparison of several choice programs, both private and public. If inherent differences in incentives to gather accurate information exist in different choice systems, it should be obvious from our data.

In fact, we found no such differences. Given that all parents surveyed can be considered active choosers, perhaps it should not be surprising that parents who selected private schools were no more likely to have knowledge about those school characteristics than MPS parents participating in the public school three-choice selection system. Or that those same parents who pay private school tuition are no more knowledgeable than parents who could merely select a district for their child rather than a specific school, as in the Milwaukee 220 program. In one instance, Milwaukee 220 parents knew more than tuition-paying private school parents—84 percent of Milwaukee 220 parents were aware of

Table 4.4. Levels of Parent Accuracy in Information

	Number of Schools	Number of Parents	Percent of Parents Who Do Not Possess Accurate Information on School Characteristic
Percent African Americans in School			
Milwaukee 220	59	81	57
Suburban 220	18	33	45
MPS	69	107	50
Citywide	30	56	55
Regular	39	51	44
Private	33	50	42
Total		271	50
Percent Reading at Grade Level			
Milwaukee 220	42	75	63
Suburban 220	16	32	47
MPS	66	104	58
Citywide	32	53	70
Regular	34	51	45
Private	NA	NA	NA
Total		211	58
Percent Eligible for Free and Reduced Lunch			
Milwaukee 220	48	96	16
Suburban 220	17	34	44
MPS	58	110	64
Citywide	23	51	71
Regular	35	59	58
Private	23	30	43
Total		270	42

the percentage of the student body of their school eligible for free or reduced-price lunch compared to 57 percent of private school parents. But for the most part, the majority of parents in both private and public school choice systems did not have accurate knowledge about their children's schools. The unanswered question is whether ignorance of details by half of the choosing parents supports entrusting school accountability to parents.[11]

Findings: A Closer Look at the Information Level of Parent Consumers

Before considering this question, we examined another means for assessing the knowledge level of parent-consumers. This entailed measuring responses to a survey question that does not pertain to specific facts about the demographic makeup of the student body or achievement level of students but merely asked for general school information. We know that in making most decisions people do not possess encyclopedic information about the matters in question (Lupia and McCubbins, 1998). Therefore, we believed it was important to examine whether parents had broad, general knowledge of the school. To do so, we asked whether parents know the name of the principal at their child's school. We did not verify if a parent was correct on this answer.[12] We trusted that a positive answer to the question meant the respondent did know the name of the principal.

We found that the majority of parents knew the name of the principal; however, there were some differences across choice systems.[13] At the high end, 88 percent of Suburban 220 parents knew the name of the principal compared to 83 percent of private school parents, 61 percent of Milwaukee 220 parents, 62 percent of MPS Citywide parents, and 58 percent of MPS Regular parents.

Several things are apparent from these data. Between 10 and 40 percent of parents in the different choice programs do not know the names of the principals in their children's schools. Second, the difference in knowledge levels does not correlate with being a public or private school parent. Private school parents and Suburban 220 parents who choose a Milwaukee public school are equally likely to possess knowledge about this school fact. Third, the differences do not vary by whether a parent selects a district or a particular school. Milwaukee 220 parents, who can select only a school district, are just as likely to know the name of the principal as parents who participate in the MPS three-choice selection process. In light of these findings it is important to again highlight that all parents surveyed can be considered active choosers. For this reason, perhaps our expectations should be that their knowledge about their school would be similar. The data appear to support this assertion.

Because support for parental accountability hinges on the belief that choice empowers parents to gather information, it is important to examine whether the disparities we find in general school knowledge are due to differences in the choice programs or to other characteristics of the parent. To test the hypothesis that it is the choice program itself that matters, we developed a logistic regression model that analyzes the probability of knowing the name of the principal while controlling for other variables that may help explain the variation in this knowledge.

The independent variables that could help explain the variation in knowledge levels include the parent's race, educational level, household income, church attendance, and length of residence in the district. The race and/or ethnic group variable was coded one if the parent is white, zero if not.[14] The education variable was coded one for parents who have a four-year college degree or higher, zero if not.[15] Our income variable was coded into eight separate categories from "Under $10,000" to "Above $70,000."[16] Church attendance ranged from "Attend more than once a week" to "Never attend."[17] Length of residence in the district was a continuous variable measuring years in the district.[18]

The results demonstrate a statistically significant difference between two choice programs (table 4.5).[19] Milwaukee 220 parents are the

Table 4.5. Logistic Regression Model of Knowledge of Principal by Different Forms of Choice

	Coefficient	Standard Error	Chi-Square	Log Odds Ratio Estimates
Intercept	1.08	0.22	23.52**	
Type of choice[1]				
Milwaukee 220	−0.42	0.21	4.06*	0.45
MPS Citywide	−0.42	0.27	2.42	0.52
MPS Regular	−0.29	0.25	1.38	0.46
Suburban 220	0.76	0.46	2.73	1.5
Education				
Less than college degree	−0.29	0.14	4.52*	0.56
Nonwhite	−0.38	0.14	7.17**	0.47
Length of time in district	0.008	0.01	0.4	
Church attendance[2]				
More than once a week	0.73	0.26	8.01**	4.7
Once a week	0.05	0.2	0.07	2.4
Less than once a week but at least once a month	0.007	0.24	0.001	2.3
Less than once a month but at least once a year	−0.03	0.29	0.01	2.2
More than once a year	0.06	0.48	0.02	2.4
Household income[3]				
$0–10,999	−0.34	0.37	0.87	0.7
$11,000–19,999	−0.08	0.28	0.07	0.92
$20,000–29,999	−0.37	0.24	2.42	0.68
$30,000–39,999	0.29	0.28	1.09	1.3
$40,000–49,999	−0.03	0.28	0.01	0.96
$50,000–59,999	0.12	0.3	0.16	1
$60,000–69,999	0.39	0.4	0.92	1.5
Likelihood ratio chi-square test statistic	74.94	19 df	0.0001	
Somers' D	0.48			

Note: Dependent variable is 1 indicating individual knows principals name

[1] Reference group for log odds ratio is parents in tuition-based choice
[2] Reference group for log odds ratio are parents who are not church attendees
[3] Reference group for log odds ratio are respondents with income >$70,000

* p. < .05   ** p. < .01

only group that is significantly different from private school parents after controlling for the individual characteristics of the parent.[20] We used a statistic called the log odds ratio to measure the likelihood of a parent having knowledge of the principal as compared to a parent in the reference group (private school parents).[21] The log odds ratio of .45 denotes that knowledge of the principal's name is nearly half as likely among Milwaukee 220 parents as among parents in tuition-based private school. There are no other significant variations between parents in any of the other choice systems and private school parents. We do find, however, that nonwhite parents and parents without a college degree are half as likely to know the names of their children's principals as white parents and college-educated parents, respectively. Finally, parents who attend church more than once a week are four and a half times more likely than parents who never attend church to know the names of their children's principals. Interestingly, parents who attend church more than once a week are just as likely to have their children enrolled in public school as in private school, therefore diminishing any anticipated connection between church attendance and knowledge of a private school.

Thus, in terms of general knowledge levels, the type of choice program matters in only one case. Parents who participate in traditional tuition-based private school choice are more likely to know the name of their children's principals than parents whose children attend suburban public schools under the Chapter 220 program. After controlling for race and education, we find no significant differences in knowledge level between parents who select private school and parents who select MPS. Therefore, with one exception, the parents choosing in the most marketlike choice system—traditional tuition-based private school—have no greater tendency to gather accurate information than parents choosing in a public school choice system.

Overall, in these first two examinations of school knowledge we find that a large number of parents are uninformed about the schools their children attend. Fewer than half of the parents surveyed possess accurate information on specific school characteristics such as student achievement and student makeup. More parents do possess general information about the school, but, in contrast to our hypothesis, differences in general knowledge levels appear to be more a factor of race, education, or church attendance than the type of choice system. The case can be made that since parents in all choice systems are rather uninformed about their children's schools, additional accountability mechanisms are necessary to ensure adequate information is available for all of a parent's schooling options.

Findings: The Consistency of the Signals Parents Send When Choosing

We examined parents' knowledge levels based on characteristics we think demonstrate adequate information about a school. Some may argue, however, that parents may not be interested in these characteristics and perhaps should not be expected to know about factors they do not deem important in a school. Thus, the next step in our analysis looked at what parents viewed as the important factors when selecting a school and how they communicated these factors to other parents and to other schools in the marketplace. The survey data indicate how clear these signals are, that is, whether parents actually sought information on the factors they said were important to them in selecting a school. For accountability to function accurately based on the actions of informed parent-consumers, parents should send clear messages about what they seek in a school, allowing competing schools to react and relay their responses to other parents. Ultimately, those schools that meet parents' desired characteristics should prosper, and those that do not will close.

In order to understand whether or not parents are sending consistent signals, we asked parents if they requested information on several factors when choosing a school. We then compared those responses with the three factors they felt were the most important when choosing a school. The question on what factors were important was open-ended. The question asking if they gathered information on a particular question was closed-ended. For this reason, it was not possible to ask respondents if they gathered information on every important variable. The closed-ended question included those categories that we hypothesized would be very important in selecting a school. If we had been able to ask the data-gathering question for all thirty-five categories mentioned by parents, the likelihood of getting mixed signals would have increased. The closed-ended question on obtaining information read, "Did you obtain any of the following information on any of the schools you applied to?" The list included student achievement, class size, teacher qualifications, administrator/principal qualifications, what is being taught, method of teaching, incidents of discipline at the school, special programs, incidents of safety at the school, opportunities for parental involvement, and athletics and other extracurricular activities.

A mixed signal results where the parent indicated a variable was an important factor when choosing a school but did not gather information on it. For example, the interviewee with ID number 8 mentioned that what is taught at the school, safety and discipline at the school, and the administrators' qualifications were the three most important factors in choosing a school. But respondent 8 did not seek information on administrators or discipline at the school; therefore, this respondent presented a mixed signal. If a respondent did not gather information on any one of the three characteristics they deemed important in a school, the response was categorized as a mixed signal. Likewise, if a respondent did not gather information on more than one characteristic they deemed important we did not weight that as a higher-level mixed signal. Parents either gave a mixed signal or they did not.

There are two ways of interpreting the data presented in table 4.6. The first conclusion is that there is a remarkable degree of consistency between what parents say they look for in a school and what data

Table 4.6. Number of Consistent and Mixed Signals when Gathering Information on Important Factors in a School

	Consistent Signals: Sought information on factors parents said were important in selecting a school		Mixed Signals: Did *not* seek information on factors parents said were important in selecting a school		
	Number	Percent	Number	Percent	Total
Milwaukee 220	124	65	67	35	191
MPS	151	79	39	21	190
Citywide	59	79	16	21	75
Regular	92	80	23	20	115
Suburban 220	53	87	8	13	61
Private	138	78	38	22	176
Total	466	75	152	25	618

they gather on a school. Depending on the choice program, between 65 and 87 percent of all parents are actually gathering information about a school based on the factors important to them. The second conclusion is that the mixed signals are troublesome. Mixed signals cause one to question how parents can hold schools accountable when they do not actually seek information about the factors they say are important in a school.

To find out whether the differences in the frequency of mixed signals are related to the type of choice program or to individual characteristics of the parents, we again used logistic regression, analyzing the same demographic variables as the previous analysis. We find parents who participate in the Milwaukee 220 program are more likely to send mixed signals than parents whose children attend traditional tuition-paying private schools (table 4.7).[22] An examination of the log odds ratio estimates reveals that the occurrence of a consistent signal is one-third as frequent among Milwaukee 220 parents as it is among parents who choose tuition-based private schools. However, there are no significant

Table 4.7. Logistic Regression Model of Different Forms of Choice and Gathering Information on Important Factors in a School

	Coefficient	Standard Error	Chi-Square	Log Odds Ratio Estimates
Intercept	1.45	0.21	47.31**	
Type of choice[1]				
Milwaukee 220	−0.86	0.2	18.25**	0.34
MPS Citywide	0.16	0.28	0.33	0.93
MPS Regular	−0.1	0.25	0.16	0.72
Suburban 220	0.57	0.37	2.41	1.4
Education				
Less than college degree	−0.15	0.13	1.36	0.75
Nonwhite	0.21	0.14	2.5	1.5
Length of time in district	−0.006	0.01	0.27	
Church attendance[2]				
More than once a week	−0.02	0.24	0.005	1.1
Once a week	0.09	0.2	0.25	1.2
Less than once a week but at least once a month	−0.03	0.23	0.01	1.1
Less than once a month but at least once a year	0.09	0.29	0.1	1.2
More than once a year	−0.06	0.43	0.02	1
Household income[3]				
$0–10,999	0.56	0.5	1.24	2
$11,000–19,999	0.39	0.32	1.42	1.7
$20,000–29,999	−0.59	0.24	6.08**	0.63
$30,000–39,999	−0.24	0.26	0.89	0.89
$40,000–49,999	−0.03	0.27	0.01	1
$50,000–59,999	−0.45	0.27	2.85	0.72
$60,000–69,999	0.5	0.39	1.67	1.9
N = 516				
Likelihood ratio chi-square test statistic	34.8	19 df	0.01	
Somers' D	0.33			

Dependent variable is 1 indicating individual consistently gathered information on factors they said were important in selecting a school. A negative coefficient suggests individuals possessing characteristics were less likely to be consistent.

[1] Reference group for log odds ratio is parents in tuition based choice

[2] Reference group for log odds ratio are parents who are not church attendees

[3] Reference group for log odds ratio are respondents with income >$70,000

* p. < .05   ** p. < .01

differences between private school parents and other public school parents. All other individual characteristics of the parents are insignificant except for income; church attendance, race, and length of time in the district are not significantly related to sending mixed signals.[23]

The question remains whether an education market provides enough incentives for gathering information and sending clear, consistent signals to entrust accountability entirely to parent-consumers. The number of consumers who are informed and send consistent signals in the education marketplace varies; but in only one case is this variation related to the type of choice program. This is true of all our tests of the existence of informed and consistent consumers—knowledge of school characteristics, knowledge of principal, and clarity of signals—implying that the degree to which choice provides sufficient incentive for parents to gather information for holding schools accountable is limited.

Conclusion

School choice has the potential to empower parents to collect information about schools and select schools on the basis of the factors that are important to them. Choice thereby offers the opportunity for parents, rather than the government, to be ultimately responsible for holding schools accountable. Schools that meet parents' desires will succeed and the others will fail.

Achieving accountability of this nature requires that parents possess adequate information about the schools they chose. In addition, it requires the signals parents send when they select a school to be clear. We hypothesized that in choice systems, where there are few outside accountability mechanisms, parents would have greater incentive to gather accurate information and would be more consistent in the messages they deliver to the schools and to other parents. We expected to find more informed parent-consumers in traditional tuition-based private schools than in the various public school choice systems because the private school system operates most like a true market.

Instead, we find choice systems differ only slightly in the extent to which they motivate parents to seek information. We are no more likely to find informed and consistent consumers in traditional tuition-based private school choice than in public school choice systems, with one exception—parents sending their children from Milwaukee to suburban public schools through an interdistrict integration program. In terms of general knowledge of a school we find that such individual characteristics of a parent as race, education, and church attendance matter more.

Therefore, it seems clear that structuring a school choice system on the pure competitive market theory that well-informed, knowledgeable parents and their resulting actions are all that is necessary to hold such schools accountable falls short in the reality of the Milwaukee experience. Private school parents, who are most comparable to voucher parents and who could be expected to have a deeper interest in their schools than public school parents for whom outside accountability mechanisms already exist, are no better informed or consistent in their behavior than their public school counterparts. At this point the market theory does not hold to its promise of accountability.

CHAPTER FIVE

Shopping for Schools

A t the heart of the choice movement is a belief that by letting
parents select their schools, we empower parents to become consumers of education. As with any big ticket item, it is hypothesized that parents will shop around for schools for their children and
will select schools based on the criteria they deem important. Schools
will succeed or fail based on their responsiveness to parents' desires.

Yet we know that most parents are uninformed about their children's schools. The previous chapter demonstrated that most parents do
not possess information on specific school characteristics and over a
third cannot provide general information on their child's school, such
as the name of the school's principal. Even more, a number of parents
do not actually obtain information on characteristics they consider most
important when selecting a school. How can this lack of knowledge be
reconciled with a school choice system in which the actions of parents
are deemed to be the primary means for holding schools accountable?

Parents as Shoppers

Some critics might argue that a parent's lack of recall knowledge about a particular school characteristic need not be distressing.
After all, our conclusions about parents' knowledge are based on surveys

in which we have essentially quizzed parents regarding specific characteristics and then scored them on their accuracy. Some might believe
that this is not a fair assessment, for, as we know from survey research,
most people simply cannot recall information on specific issues. For
example, previous research has shown that people lack specific information on most political issues (Lupia and McCubbins 1998; Delli, Carpini,
and Keeter 1996) yet still decide for whom to vote. Perhaps choosing a
school works in the same way.

Others point out that parents select schools in ways that have
nothing to do with specific characteristics of the school. Personal net-
works, friends, family, and church play an important role in providing
information on education options (Carver and Salganik 1991; Witte 1994:
4). Parents essentially learn from others who possess more knowledge
about the schools than they do, the most prevalent being friends and
relatives. Others point out that minority parents and parents of lower
socioeconomic status have fewer interactions with individuals who have
knowledge about schools and therefore possess less knowledge about
them (Schneider, Teske, and Marshall 2000: chap. 5; Henig 1996).

To address these criticisms we consider a different method for
understanding how much information parents have when making
schooling choices. We observe parents as they are "shopping" for
schools. We do this because despite the fact that parents may learn about
schools from others, or the fact that they may not need specific assessment or performance information in selecting a school, there is still
a need to obtain school-based information if parents' choices are to
adequately hold schools accountable.

Currently, despite the need for a clear understanding of the
shopping experiences of parents, virtually nothing is known about these
experiences. There is, however, a solid understanding of what parents
say they want to know about a school.

When surveyed, parents are consistent in the kind of information they say they want about a school. For example, Schneider et al.

(2000, 1998), in a study of public school choice in New York City, explore the question of whether parents make good choices given the levels of information they have. When presented with a list of school attributes that previous research had demonstrated parents care about and then asked to choose which of those attributes they thought was the most important, the majority of parents wanted information on the quality of teachers, school safety, reading and math achievement, and discipline. A study conducted by Greene et al. (1997) found similar results. Participants and applicants at the Cleveland Scholarship Program were asked, "How important were the following considerations in your decision to apply for a scholarship?" Eighty-five percent of the parents new to choice schools said they wanted to "improve the academic quality" of their child's education. Second in importance was the "greater safety" to be found at a choice school, cited by 70 percent of the recipients. Location was ranked third, and religion fourth (26–27).[1]

Our own survey research of parents in the cities of Milwaukee, Baltimore, and Denver confirms these results. In a survey of 750 parents conducted in the winter of 2001, we found parents across all three districts were primarily interested in curriculum, student achievement, location, teaching methods, and teacher qualifications (Van Dunk 2001). A Public Policy Forum survey of parents conducted in 1999 under contract with the MPS district also found student achievement, curriculum, and teacher performance to be the most important factors when choosing a school. These factors were closely followed in importance by discipline/school safety, teaching methods, class size, and the peer group. Both our own and other research has shown that parents are highly consistent when asked which characteristics are most important to them in choosing a school.

But are parents able to gather information about the factors they find important in a school? To examine this question we chose a different approach from most recent research on school choice: we used a method termed role-based participant observation. We "joined" parents as they visited schools to examine whether, as shoppers, they can gather enough information to hold schools accountable.

Methodology

In a choice system like Milwaukee's, in which there is no formal outside accountability mechanism, parents cannot compare voucher schools on the basis of such school-based data as teacher qualifications, curriculum, graduation rate, retention, and test scores. And because the information is simply not available, not even a parent's network of friends and relatives is a useful source. For these reasons, one of the most productive ways for parents to learn about voucher schools is to visit them. Visiting allows a parent to inspect the facilities, to receive information about curriculum and teaching, and, most important, to decide whether this particular school fits the needs of his or her child. The parent can judge with his or her own eyes whether the school is a good choice. As a result, if a school is to survive it should be responsive to consumers. It would seem axiomatic that in a competitive education marketplace, schools hoping to succeed would do their best to accommodate the parents of prospective students who are visiting the school and to present themselves in the best light possible.

Visiting schools is critical not only to selecting a child's school but also for ultimately holding schools accountable, since visiting should allow a parent to make an objective assessment of the school. Despite this important role of school shopping, there are no studies analyzing whether school visitation is a realistic means of holding schools accountable. To fill this gap, we used parent-researchers to learn about the school shopping process. We chose this methodology of role-based participant observation because the database of actual Milwaukee voucher parents is not open to the public.[2]

The Public Policy Forum hired seven parent-researchers to visit forty-one voucher schools and twelve public schools in January 2001.

Six of our parent-researchers were undergraduate or graduate students at the University of Wisconsin–Milwaukee (UWM), and the seventh was an undergraduate student at Mount Mary College.[3] They were chosen primarily because they were parents of school-age children and/or interested in role-based participant research.[4] The staff of the Public Policy Forum conducted a training session during which a school visit protocol form was reviewed and the parent-researchers were given a list of questions to ask at each school. The questions were designed to be typical questions parents would ask upon visiting a school for the first time. They were based on information we obtained from face-to-face interviews with Milwaukee voucher parents in 1997 and on a school visit protocol used by Teske and his coauthors in their 2000 study of Washington, D.C., charter schools (Van Dunk 1998).[5]

Often role-based participant observation involves unannounced participation, in which the subjects being observed are unaware of the participation of the researcher. For example, unannounced observation is commonly used by fair housing organizations to test for housing discrimination by having researchers play the role of potential renters or buyers. And while role-based observation is rare in school choice research, Teske et al. (2000) used unannounced observation when visiting charter schools in Washington, D.C., with parent-researchers. Although we support the research validity of unannounced observation, we decided to announce our purpose during our visits. Our school visit protocol called for each parent-researcher to provide the school with her name and her affiliation with the Public Policy Forum as a parent-researcher. Our parent-researchers were also instructed to share information about the Forum if someone from the school asked.

The decision to announce our research objective when visiting was based on several criteria. First, while unannounced observation may be the best way to fully understand some issues, such as discrimination, we did not feel that announcing our purpose would affect our results. Most voucher schools know the Forum as a leading place for parents to obtain information about the choice program and the participating schools and are not wary of our research.[6] Second, we did not feel that announcing our parent-researchers' affiliation with the Forum would compromise the shopping experience. Our parent-researchers were truly interested in visiting schools for the sake of their children or of their families' and friends' children. Their interest in reporting their experiences to us was only secondary to their interest in visiting potential schools for these children. Third, we felt it was important to the integrity of the Forum as a research organization that we announce these visits. We felt that if we did not announce our visits, we might jeopardize future data collection efforts at the schools. The announcing of our visits was not without some repercussions. We received two phone calls, one from a public school administrator and another from a private school administrator, regarding our parent-researcher visits. We informed the callers that the anonymity of all the schools would be respected when our findings were reported.

The parent-researchers selected the voucher schools they wanted to visit from a representative sample of all private schools participating in the choice program. Their selections were based on criteria such as the age and gender of the parent-researcher's child(ren) and the parent-researcher's religion, race or ethnicity, and area of residence. Each parent-researcher selected between one and eleven schools. On average, each parent visited eight schools, six private voucher schools and two randomly selected Milwaukee public schools. We included visits to public schools so that the researchers might obtain a full experience of shopping for schools in the city of Milwaukee; our intent was not to compare the public school visits with the private school visits.[7]

Before the visiting began, we provided the parent-researchers with some basic data we had compiled about each school, that is, location, grade levels, and religious affiliation.[8] We did not give them information regarding the choice program because they were not to play the role of voucher parents. From conversations with actual voucher parents, we knew it would be unlikely for a parent to indicate that they are seeking a voucher during their first visit to a school (Van Dunk 2001a). This is primarily because few parents are aware at the time they are shopping for a school whether their financial situation warrants qualification for a voucher. We did instruct our parent-researchers to ask for information about financial aid and to note whether the school mentioned the choice program.

Our main purpose was to investigate how much a parent can learn about a school by visiting it. Information is a necessary component of accountability. We developed standard guidelines for our parent-researchers that focused on the two main kinds of information one would expect to receive during a school visit: (1) information about the school's facilities, and (2) information about the school's educational programing.

While gathering information about schools' facilities, the parent-researchers were asked to specifically pay attention to the safety of the street, the state of repair of the school building, signs of graffiti or vandalism outside and inside the school building, the cleanliness of the entranceway and hallways, and whether student work was displayed in the halls. Parental impressions of school facilities are important because when complete information about school characteristics is not available, parents may use shortcuts in determining school quality. Schneider et al. (2000: chap. 8) explored this process by focusing on visual cues that may reduce a parent's desire for specific knowledge about a school, for example, a school with graffiti on the walls may be perceived as a low-performing school. To examine what impressions parents draw about a school from its physical appearance and surroundings, we asked our parent-visitors to assess the appearance of the school and neighborhood.

The school's facilities and neighborhood may offer useful clues, but most parents visiting schools are trying to learn about the school's educational program. Our parent-researchers asked school personnel to describe a typical day or week for a student in the grade level of the child for whom they were doing the shopping. Parent-researchers reported whether and how well the school staff explained the teaching approach, curriculum, student achievement, and teachers' qualifications. In addition, the parent-researchers noted whether and how the school explained its application procedure, financial aid (including vouchers), and school policies such as school uniforms, discipline, parental involvement, and religious participation. The parent-researchers also noted whether the school staff informed them about the demographic makeup of the student body and whether they were allowed to observe children in their classrooms.

After each visit, we asked our parent-researchers, "Do you feel you received enough information to make a choice about the school?" Whether the choice was positive or negative did not matter, only whether they felt they could make an informed choice after having visited the school.

Sample of Schools

The sample of 41 private voucher schools visited by our parent-researchers represents the entire population of 103 Milwaukee voucher schools in existence in 2000–01. This ensures that our findings are generalizable to the broader community of voucher schools. As shown in table 5.1, the schools the researchers selected are representative as to the following characteristics: total school enrollment, voucher student enrollment, the ratio of voucher enrollment to overall enrollment, grade levels offered, religious affiliation, years in existence, years participating in MPCP, and location.

Findings: Shopping for Schools Is Not an Easy Task

Before discussing what information parents who are school shopping can obtain by visiting voucher schools, we first make note of

Table 5.1. Selected Characteristics of Sampled Schools vs. Population of MPCP Schools

Number of Full-time Equivalent Voucher Students

	0–19	20–39	40–59	60–79	80–99	100–129	130–159	160–199	200–299	≧300
Sample number	8	9	5	7	2	5	2	2	2	2
Percent of sample	18.2%	20.5%	11.4%	15.9%	4.5%	11.4%	4.5%	4.5%	4.5%	4.5%
Percent of all schools	14.6%	20.4%	12.6%	17.5%	5.8%	7.8%	5.8%	5.8%	4.9%	4.9%

Percent of Total Enrollment that are Voucher Students

	≦10	11–20	21–40	41–60	61–80	81–99	100
Sample number	6	2	7	7	11	7	4
Percent of sample	13.6%	4.5%	15.9%	15.9%	25.0%	15.9%	9.1%
Percent of all schools	10.7%	4.8%	15.5%	20.4%	22.3%	18.4%	5.8%

Grades Served

	Kindergarten only	K–3d	K–6th	K–8th	6th–8th	High School	K–12th
Sample number	3	6	5	24	1	3	2
Percent of sample	6.8%	13.6%	11.4%	54.5%	2.3%	6.8%	4.5%
Percent of all schools	5.8%	10.7%	11.6%	58.3%	2.9%	6.8%	3.9%

Religious Affiliation

	Catholic	Lutheran	Christian Nondenominational	Other Christian	Islamic	Jewish	None
Sample number	13	6	6	4	1	1	13
Percent of sample	29.5%	13.6%	13.6%	9.1%	2.3%	2.3%	29.5%
Percent of all schools	36.9%	14.6%	8.7%	18.4%	1.9%	1.0%	27.2%

Location

	North	NW	South	SW	West	Eastside/Downtown
Sample number	9	16	9	2	6	2
Percent of sample	20.5%	36.4%	20.5%	4.5%	13.6%	4.5%
Percent of all schools	19.4%	36.9%	21.4%	4.9%	14.6%	2.9%

Teske and his coauthors (2000) found in Washington, D.C., that charter schools have a better environment than traditional public schools. Specifically, they note that more than 10 percent of the Washington, D.C., public schools had broken windows, and more than 20 percent were marked by graffiti. They report that none of these conditions were found in D.C. charter schools.

Evaluation of the schools' facilities by our parent-researchers shows that the majority of the visited schools are located on safe streets (table 5.2). Only five of the schools had boarded-up or abandoned buildings nearby. The majority of schools were thought to be in safe locations. On a scale of one (not safe) to ten (safe), the perceived safety of the schools' locations averaged eight, just five schools (12.5 percent) being rated between one and four.

It is difficult to know how to interpret data assessing the perceived safety of the neighborhood surrounding the school. After all, schools have little control over the security or upkeep of their neighborhoods except for the initial site selection. Our findings suggest that visitors to most of the voucher schools' neighborhoods would have a good first impression. Yet some of Milwaukee's greatest educational needs are in areas of the city that many would consider blighted and neglected. A good school in one of these "bad" neighborhoods would be a blessing. For this reason, while we continue to include measures of the surrounding neighborhood in our analysis, we want to point out our apprehension about using such a measure to assess how much information parents have about voucher schools. Perhaps a better measure of perception is the condition of the school building itself, over which schools do have direct control.

To examine school building conditions, our parent-researchers had to enter the school facility. Once inside, they either were offered or asked for a tour of the school. On a scale of one (bad repair) to ten (good repair), the average condition of the school buildings was 7.9, with five schools ranked five or below. Just two schools had broken

The school was excellent, with a wonderful curriculum and a beautiful learning facility, but for a parent with limited time, learning about the school and the curriculum would be a task."

The only way to truly allow parents to take advantage of the power of their choices is to make sure they can easily exercise all their options. We found that if parents lack determination or time, they may not be able to obtain information about all their schooling options.

Findings: First Impression of School Facilities and Neighborhood

We felt it was important to assess the visual shopping experience of parents because other school choice researchers have attempted to show that visual impressions are used to form opinions about actual school performance, whether true or not (Schneider et al. 1999). This kind of decision making is not limited to school choice. In the field of criminal justice the belief that neglected neighborhoods are more likely to be places of high crime has moved entire city police departments to reexamine the way they deal with crime. In fact, in Milwaukee, Wilson and Kelling's (1982) "broken window" philosophy has been the main operational theory of the police department since 1997. At its core the broken window theory is quite simple: if areas of the city are neglected— graffiti are not cleaned up, abandoned buildings are allowed to stand, garbage is not collected, petty crimes are tolerated—citizens will perceive these areas to be unsafe. Such an image will deter people from moving to them, leading to a type of self-fulfilling prophecy. Only individuals unable to relocate or those with criminal intent will continue to stay in the neglected neighborhood.

Where schools are concerned, the belief is that a visual impression can afford an accurate means of assessing the performance of the school. In other words, even if parents rely only on visual cues, they can still make a reliable assessment of the school's educational quality.

Figure 5.1. The Ease of Shopping for Schools

Finding the Entrance
    23 schools—easy to find entrance
    15 schools—difficult to find entrance

Entering the School
    26 schools—locked door with buzzer and directions
    7 schools—unlocked door with no directions
    4 schools—locked door with no directions
    1 school—unlocked door with greeter to provide directions

Waiting to be Helped
    23 schools—waited 3 minutes or less
    13 schools—waited 4 to 10 minutes
    2 schools—waited 11 to 15 minutes

Asking for Help
    27 schools—staff responsive to questions
    11 schools—staff unresponsive to questions

Taking a Tour
    16 schools—offered a tour
    14 schools—provided tour after being asked
    5 schools—required appointment for tour
    3 schools—declined request for tour

Making a Second Visit
    35 schools—second visit not required
    3 schools—second visit was required before information was obtained
    3 schools—unable to obtain information even after two visits

Staff Demeanor
    31 schools—courteous
    7 schools—not courteous

schools make finding the entrance simple, in more than a dozen schools this was not the case. In some instances every step, from finding the entrance to taking a tour, took great determination (fig. 5.1). Because of these barriers, some parents may simply be overwhelmed by the effort required to perform even the most basic information gathering. Because our parent-researchers were being paid to report on their experiences they may have been better motivated to complete their visits. Parents who do not have such motivation may well be discouraged upon finding a locked door, no signs, an unresponsive staff member, or upon being told they need to return for a second visit. Many parents encountering such obstacles at a school may just leave empty-handed.

Visiting schools during the school day is time-consuming. On average our researchers spent approximately two hours visiting a school. The average length of the interior visit to each school was forty minutes, ranging from zero to one hour forty minutes. The remainder of the time was employed in travel and observation of the exterior of the school. To treat parents poorly or even expect them to make the trip more than once does not seem to be in a school's best interest. Nor is it in a school's best interest to make it difficult or intimidating for the parent of a prospective student to enter the school and find the office. Yet our parent-researchers found that a number of private voucher schools are not competing to provide the best "customer service" to visitors; many schools do not even seem to realize they should woo prospective parents. Unfortunately, when making their choices, parents cannot just assume that a school with poor customer service is not a quality school. One of our parent-researchers summed this up best when she wrote of her difficulty in visiting a school: "When I first visited I was just given a packet and told to schedule a visit; however, scheduling the tour was difficult. I thought I would be able to call and go in a day or two, but when I called, the woman in charge of scheduling tours was out sick. So I had to wait for her to call me back and then I was able to go in.

entry, finding a locked door would likely not be discouraging to most visiting parents because safety is an important concern.

After entering a school, our parent-researchers were to estimate how long they had to wait before being helped. The wait ranged from zero to fifteen minutes; most parent-researchers reported they did not have to wait at all. The average wait was three minutes. Therefore, once parent-researchers had reached the school office, the schools seemed eager to welcome them. Our parent-researchers reported they found responsive staffs at 72 percent of the schools. One said, "The teachers were all very friendly towards my daughter and took the time to tell us about their day and answer questions." While this was the typical experience, another 28 percent of the school officials were unresponsive to requests for information.

Most school representatives treated our parent-researchers very courteously. On a scale of zero (not at all) to ten (very courteously) of how courteously they were treated, parent-researchers gave the schools they visited an average of eight, with more schools (43 percent) scoring a ten than any other score. Seven of the school staffs were given a courtesy score of seven or less.

We asked our parent-researchers to note whether anyone at the school offered them a tour or whether they had to ask for a tour. Sixteen schools offered a tour without being asked, while twenty-two did not. Of those twenty-two, eight refused to give a tour after being requested to do so. One of these schools stated that tours are given only if the child is admitted. Five schools declined but suggested the parent-researcher make an appointment to return for a tour. Two school administrators flatly declined to give a tour, and at one school the tour was not given because, owing to a teacher conference, no teachers or students were present.

The reports from our parent-researchers indicate that shopping among voucher schools can be a difficult task. While the majority of dark and locked. The second visit a lady asked me in and said that I had to make an appointment."

We asked our parent-researchers to rate the ease with which they found the entrance to the school building. On a scale of zero (very hard to find) to ten (easily identified), on average the voucher schools visited scored a seven. Eleven schools, or 28 percent, scored a ten; 10 percent scored a nine; and 20 percent scored an eight; in total, 83 percent scored a six or above. Difficulty in finding access to a building was the exception. Yet parent-researchers found it extremely hard to gain access to six buildings. In two of these instances access was scored at zero because the entrance was never found. Sometimes the difficulty in finding the school entrance resulted from the school's being housed in a church. Parent-researchers often found it problematic to find the school entrance among the various church entrances, especially if the school operated in the basement of the church building. Other schools seemed to have more than one entrance, but actually used only one door, which commonly was not the most obvious or did not correlate to the school's address. In at least three instances the school's entrance was not marked with signage of any kind.

Once the proper entrance was found, it was common to find the door locked. For security reasons, this should be expected. At twenty-six of the schools visited, the doors were locked, and visitors had to use a buzzer or knock until someone let them in. One parent-researcher reported that she had to knock very hard until "eventually some men doing work on the building went and got someone to let us in." Only one school had an unlocked door with a greeter posted inside to guide visitors to their destination. Seven schools had unlocked doors but no information on how to find the administrative offices. At the remaining four schools our parent-researchers found other ways of gaining entry, for example, by following a student or parent into the building. As long as the school somehow made it apparent how to gain fornia "simply refused to provide information about their schools," and other school choice researchers who reported similar findings (Wilson 1992; Carver and Salganik 1991).

The results of our parent visits are no different. The comments regarding the visits ranged from great enthusiasm to disgust. One parent-researcher reflected on the excitement of her visit this way: "The entrance was easy to locate. The people were extremely friendly and helpful. We were given immediate assistance. We sat in the office and spoke one-on-one with the administrators. We were then given a tour of the two K4 rooms." The variation in visiting experiences is revealed in another parent-researcher's account: "I was not able to get inside of this school if there is one. It is a very old building. There is no sign of a school entrance. All church entrances are locked and no one is around. It is located in a run down residential neighborhood with a lot of boarded up houses."

We anticipated that our parent-researchers would visit forty-one private voucher schools, but in the end they gained access to only thirty-eight of the forty-one schools selected. Administrators at two schools refused to allow the parent-researchers on their premises: at one, a private religious school, the visitor was told that she could not visit the school and was sent away, and at the other, a nonreligious school, the parent-researcher was unable even to gain access. The third school, as noted above, appeared to be permanently locked and uninhabited, although the parent-researcher had called to verify the address. In addition, three schools requested that the parent-researcher return on another day after making an appointment, and two schools required the child to visit the school as well. In all, six of the voucher schools called on required more than one visit before any information about the school could be obtained from school staff. For example, one of our parent-researchers commented, "It was certainly a pain getting any information from [the school]. The first time I went the school was the intricacy of gathering information. Because DPI is unable to provide more than the school's name, address, and phone number, parents who are seeking a voucher school start at square one if they have no other connection to any of the schools. As noted, having a connection to a school through friends, family, or church is a prevalent method of learning about schools. Still, this informational source can only be as good as the information schools assemble and disseminate, which we know through years of collecting school-based data is limited compared to the vast array of information available regarding public or charter schools.[9] Three years ago the Forum began to gather basic data about voucher schools through an annual census. This information includes school size, number of voucher students, religious affiliation, availability of transportation, and before and after school care, as well as the enrollment period. We produce a poster containing these data and distribute thousands of copies of it, primarily to public libraries. Another source of data on Milwaukee schools, produced by UWM, is a website called Empowering Parents through Informed Choices in Education (EPIC). The website lists information voluntarily provided by some voucher schools, including grades offered and calendar year of the school. All of these sources are limited, however; only by calling or visiting a school can a parent obtain further information.

Our seven parent-researchers spent two weeks visiting local schools. They found great variation in their ability to enter the schools, meet with an administrator, and gather basic information. Some of the difficulties could be attributed to the fact that the visits were unscheduled and school staff may have been unprepared. In some instances, however, the school staff seemed reluctant to provide any information or allow a visitor inside the school. This reluctance appears not to be unique to Milwaukee. Schneider et al. (2000) report that other scholars have found school officials often seem to purposefully keep the costs of gathering information high, citing Henig (1994), who found that some principals participating in the Alum Rock school choice project in Cali-

Six of our parent-researchers were undergraduate or graduate students at the University of Wisconsin–Milwaukee (UWM), and the seventh was an undergraduate student at Mount Mary College.[3] They were chosen primarily because they were parents of school-age children and/or interested in role-based participant research.[4] The staff of the Public Policy Forum conducted a training session during which a school visit protocol form was reviewed and the parent-researchers were given a list of questions to ask at each school. The questions were designed to be typical questions parents would ask upon visiting a school for the first time. They were based on information we obtained from face-to-face interviews with Milwaukee voucher parents in 1997 and on a school visit protocol used by Teske and his coauthors in their 2000 study of Washington, D.C., charter schools (Van Dunk 1998).[5]

Often role-based participant observation involves unannounced participation, in which the subjects being observed are unaware of the participation of the researcher. For example, unannounced observation is commonly used by fair housing organizations to test for housing discrimination by having researchers play the role of potential renters or buyers. And while role-based observation is rare in school choice research, Teske et al. (2000) used unannounced observation when visiting charter schools in Washington, D.C., with parent-researchers. Although we support the research validity of unannounced observation, we decided to announce our purpose during our visits. Our school visit protocol called for each parent-researcher to provide the school with her name and her affiliation with the Public Policy Forum as a parent-researcher. Our parent-researchers were also instructed to share information about the Forum if someone from the school asked.

The decision to announce our research objective when visiting was based on several criteria. First, while unannounced observation may be the best way to fully understand some issues, such as discrimination, we did not feel that announcing our purpose would affect our results. Most voucher schools know the Forum as a leading place for parents

ents as they visited schools to examine whether, as shoppers, they can gather enough information to hold schools accountable.

Methodology

In a choice system like Milwaukee's, in which there is no formal outside accountability mechanism, parents cannot compare voucher schools on the basis of such school-based data as teacher qualifications, curriculum, graduation rate, retention, and test scores. And because the information is simply not available, not even a parent's network of friends and relatives is a useful source. For these reasons, one of the most productive ways for parents to learn about voucher schools is to visit them. Visiting allows a parent to inspect the facilities, to receive information about curriculum and teaching, and, most important, to decide whether this particular school fits the needs of his or her child. The parent can judge with his or her own eyes whether the school is a good choice. As a result, if a school is to survive it should be responsive to consumers. It would seem axiomatic that in a competitive education marketplace, schools hoping to succeed would do their best to accommodate the parents of prospective students who are visiting the school and to present themselves in the best light possible.

Visiting schools is critical not only to selecting a child's school but also for ultimately holding schools accountable, since visiting should allow a parent to make an objective assessment of the school. Despite this important role of school shopping, there are no studies analyzing whether school visitation is a realistic means of holding schools accountable. To fill this gap, we used parent-researchers to learn about the school shopping process. We chose this methodology of role-based participant observation because the database of actual Milwaukee voucher parents is not open to the public.[2]

The Public Policy Forum hired seven parent-researchers to visit forty-one voucher schools and twelve public schools in January 2001.

windows, three had bars on the windows, and none sported evidence
of vandalism or graffiti. In addition, on a scale of one (not clean) to
ten (clean), the entranceways and hallways scored an average of 8.5,
only two schools scored five or below. On one specific measure of the
appearance of the building, 81.5 percent of the schools had student work
displayed in hallways. Finally, we asked our parent-researchers, "Compared with other school facilities you have visited in the City of Milwaukee would you say this school is comparable, better, or worse?" Eight
of the schools were identified as worse, fifteen as comparable, and fifteen
as better.

Are first impressions based on visual indications sufficient for
holding voucher schools accountable? If our parent-researchers were
provided with no other information regarding a school, they would have
to make a decision based solely on their visual impression of the facility.
In the absence of any other information, we would have to conclude
that the fifteen voucher schools our parent-researchers felt had better
appearances than other city schools would be viewed as higher-quality
schools than the eight schools identified as worse.

But other comparative data show reliance on visual cues is a
weak means of holding schools accountable; actual voucher parents are
selecting the schools that our parent-researchers labeled worse at a similar, if not higher, rate than the schools having facilities labeled better.
The average number of voucher students in schools identified as being
in worse condition than other city schools is 83, compared to an average
of 80 voucher students at the schools in better condition. We are most
likely to find voucher students in schools considered comparable to
other city schools, where an average of 106 voucher students per school
are enrolled.

Voucher parents who do not choose a school because of its
poor appearance may therefore be missing out on a high-quality school.
Similarly, a good exterior appearance is no guarantee of what will be
found inside. At one school with a "big, beautiful, bright building with

Table 5.2. Frequencies for Characteristics of Schools' Facilities and Surroundings

Score*	Safety of Street			School Building Repair			Clean Entrance and Hallways			Facilities in Order		
	Number of Schools	Percent of Schools	Cumulative Percent	Number of Schools	Percent of Schools	Cumulative Percent	Number of Schools	Percent of Schools	Cumulative Percent	Number of Schools	Percent of Schools	Cumulative Percent
1	1	2.5	2.5	1	2.6	2.5	0	0	0	0	0	0
2	2	5	7.5	1	2.6	5.2	0	0	0	1	2.6	2.6
3	1	2.5	10	0	0	5.2	1	2.6	2.6	1	2.6	5.2
4	1	2.5	12.5	0	0	5.2	1	2.6	5.2	0	0	5.2
5	0	0	12.5	4	10.3	15.5	0	0	5.2	2	5.2	10.4
6	0	0	12.5	1	2.5	18	2	5.2	10.4	1	2.6	13
7	6	15	27.5	7	17.4	35.4	4	10.4	20.8	5	12.8	25.8
8	4	10	37.5	8	20.5	55.9	8	20.5	41.3	9	23	48.8
9	14	35	72.5	5	12.8	68.7	9	23	64.3	6	15.4	64.2
10	11	27.5	100	12	30.8	99.5**	14	35.9	100.2	14	35.9	100.1
Average score	8.02			7.8			8.2			7.9		

* Higher numbers equal more positive ratings for facilities and surroundings.
** Due to rounding numbers do not always add to 100 percent.

a very nice playground," our parent-researcher commented, "Strangely enough, the staff was completely uninterested in me. They seemed not to have the time or desire to spend time with me."

Another reason decisions based on visual cues do not lead to realistic accountability is that a school building's condition is closely linked with the year the school was founded. Of the eight schools ranked worse than other city schools, seven were founded after 1993. Three were opened in 2000. Should parents judge school quality by the year the school was founded? Although this may be possible, it would not lead to accountability because (as documented in a *New York Times* article of February 21, 2001) finding new school sites in the city of Milwaukee, as in other areas around the country, is becoming increasingly difficult. New schools may thus have high educational achievement or innovative practices while, out of necessity, being housed in facilities that appear worse than the average city school. In short, the appearance of a school tells one little about the school. Our conclusion is that using facility condition or neighborhood safety as one's sole information about a school is a poor substitute for obtaining objective, school-based information. School accountability should not rest on this type of uninformed choice.

Findings: Educational Programing and the Information Parents Desire Most

Information on educational programing and school assessment is needed if parents are to successfully hold schools accountable. Are parents offered information of this type when visiting a prospective school? Our parent-researchers recorded whether they received information on several school characteristics, chosen because they represent the characteristics parents consistently indicate are important to them in choosing a school (Greene 1997 et al.; Schneider et al. 2000; Hoxby 1999).[10] Table 5.3 shows the percentage of schools that gave information

Table 5.3. Obtaining Information on What Parents Desire Most

1. Percentage of schools that provided information on characteristics parents look for in a school

Characteristics	Percent of Schools
Curriculum	65
Student achievement	45
Teacher qualifications	26
Make-up of student body	48
Application procedure	60
Financial aid	85
Voucher program	69
School policies (including discipline, uniforms, parent involvement, and religious participation)	74

2. Index of school information

Average score from 0–9, on additive index with 9 meaning information provided on all school characteristics:	5.4

3. Parent-researchers' assessments of whether they received enough information to make a choice about the school

Average score from 0–10, with 10 meaning "Feel well informed about the school."	6.7

on each of these characteristics. The majority of schools made available information on curriculum, application procedures, financial aid, the choice program, and school policies. Parents were most likely to receive information on financial aid (85 percent). Yet considering that the schools visited were voucher schools, it is somewhat surprising that almost a third of the schools did not mention the choice program. In addition, more than a third of the schools did not instruct our parent-researchers about application procedures. Fewer than half offered information on student achievement, and teachers' qualifications proved to be the least accessible information to the parent-researchers; only 26 percent of the schools supplied this kind of information. Table 5.3 also includes the average score on an additive index for each school. The index is composed of the number of characteristics that were explained to the parent-researchers by school staff. The highest value of the index (9) indicates the school staff provided information about all the characteristics. Accordingly, an index score of eight indicates that school staff presented information on all characteristics but one. The average across all schools is 5.4.

Was the information given sufficient to enable our parent-researchers to make a decision about the school? Most schools failed to supply information about all the characteristics that previous research has determined parents deem important when choosing a school. Just six of the visited schools provided information to the parent-visitors on all of the following characteristics: curriculum/teaching approach; student achievement; teachers' qualifications; demographic makeup of the student body; the application procedure; financial aid; the choice program; school policies; and permission to observe students in their classrooms. Another ten schools presented information on seven or eight of the nine characteristics. This means that almost half of the schools supplied information on fewer than six of the nine characteristics. The fact that the other schools did provide information on at least six characteristics suggests a great deal of variation in the experiences parents will have when they shop for a school. Considering that our parent-researchers were "armed" with our protocol and guidelines, it is this variation that is worrisome. Arguably, our group of parent-researchers was better prepared for making school visits than parents who have little or no experience in school shopping. That they were unable to collect information on every characteristic from every school indicates how difficult it may be for the average parent to obtain information.

But an objective measure of how much information was obtained may not truly reflect how parents use information to make

Table 5.4. Parent-Researchers' Assessments of Whether They Received Enough Information to Make a Choice About the School

Score of the Amount of Information	Number of Schools	Percent of Schools
0	4	11
1	1	3
2	0	0
3	0	0
4	3	8
5	3	8
6	3	8
7	3	8
8	8	21
9	3	8
10	10	26

Note: 0 means "Not well informed," 10 means "Very well informed."

choices. A qualitative measure of parents' ability to make a choice is needed. Therefore, we asked our parent-researchers to assess whether they received enough information to make a choice, positive or negative, about the school. On a scale of zero (feel uninformed) to ten (feel very informed), 55 percent, or twenty-one schools, were given a score of eight or above while 29 percent, or eleven schools, were rated as five or below. Therefore, nearly two-thirds of the visits led to an informed decision about the school by the parent-researcher. As reported in table 5.4, the average score is 6.7.[11]

Does a parent-researcher's feeling about being able to make an informed decision correlate with the amount of information the school provided? In other words, does our qualitative measurement of the information provided substantiate our quantitative measurement? The correlation between the additive index measuring the amount of information provided and the qualitative measurement about feeling adequately informed is .76. Thus, the more information individuals have, the more likely they are to feel they have enough information to make a decision about the school. Knowledge is power.

But if knowledge is power, how powerful can parents' decisions be when they are not adequately informed? Our parent-researchers demonstrate that the amount of information obtained from voucher schools differs greatly among the schools. In about one-third of the visits, voucher parents may have to make decisions without much information about the school. For example, potential voucher parents will often not receive information on two of the characteristics most parents feel are important when choosing a school, teacher qualifications and student achievement—fewer than half of the schools we visited provided information on these characteristics. Yet, despite lacking this information, parents *are* making choices to send their children to these schools; last year more than thirty-four hundred voucher students were enrolled in the schools we visited. When objective, school-based information is unavailable, these parents must be relying on other means for making their decisions. They may be relying on visual cues of the interior and exterior of the school. It is more likely they are relying on family and friends for information about schools. Our research does not allow us to draw conclusions about how individual decisions regarding schooling choices are made. But it does draw into question how decisions made in the absence of readily available, school-based information can be relied on to hold schools accountable to everyone.

Conclusion

The experiences of our parent-researchers indicate great variability among voucher schools in their ability or willingness to provide information and serve their prospective "customers." Approximately one-third of the schools made it incredibly difficult to obtain information from them. Additionally, even after visiting the school, parents in over half the schools left without information on academic performance and teacher qualifications. Whether or not schools put up these barriers to information intentionally or unknowingly, the result is the same— some parents will be forced to make a schooling decision with little school-based information.

Many of these parents may rely on such perceptions as visual cues. This kind of information, however, results in less informed parental choices. If school choice is only about allowing parents to choose, then this is of no concern. But if school choice is about empowering parents so they can improve education, then uninformed choices are a serious blow to the belief that accountability should be solely the responsibility of parents. Unfortunately, in Milwaukee, voucher schools are not always providing information to parents as they shop—and there is no other objective resource parents can go to for the missing information. Information about educational options must be more easily available to all if parents are to hold schools accountable by making informed schooling decisions for their children.

CHAPTER SIX

Do the Dollars Follow the Child?

T he market theory of competition in education hinges on the assumption that all schools will be subject to the effects of the marketplace. During legislative debates about the MPCP, school choice proponents argued that the dollars would follow the child from a bad school to a better school, thereby rewarding success while penalizing poor performance. As explained by Wisconsin governor Tommy Thompson's chief of staff, John Matthews, in the *Milwaukee Journal* for January 15, 1995, "The state's resources are paid to parents, and the parents choose where that money flows from there."

In this chapter, we approach the issue of parent actions and accountability from a fiscal perspective. Unlike most studies of voucher costs, we are not trying to determine whether, from a fiscal perspective, vouchers would be good public policy (or whether voucher schools do more with less). We are examining a system in which vouchers *are* public policy, and we wish to determine whether they have the fiscal impact on schools on which they are premised (that is, do the dollars follow the child?). If the dollars do not follow the child, if schools are insulated from the full impact of market forces, then choice will not spur competition for money. Additionally, when the dollars cannot be traced directly to parents' choices, taxpayers and policymakers cannot determine how public funds are being used. Therefore, our third prong of accountability hinges on the fiscal impacts to competing schools. Parents plainly cannot hold schools accountable if their choices do not have a clear financial consequence.

The MPCP Funding Mechanism

Equalization Aid

In the past decade, Wisconsin has shifted the burden of education funding from local property tax rolls to the state by committing to fund two-thirds of K–12 education costs with state funds. Since this shift the formula used to distribute general state education aid is an equalization formula, which the DPI characterizes as an attempt to eliminate school districts' differences in *ability* to spend on education, while still allowing for variation in school districts' *willingness* to spend on education (Van Dunk 2000). To accomplish this, the state provides equalization aid, but also sets a revenue limit for each school district's tax levy, which cannot be surpassed unless a district's voters pass a special referendum.

The amount of equalization aid distributed to a school district is based on five factors: (1) membership, or the number of full-time pupils enrolled in a school district, (2) shared costs, or a school district's incurred costs that are eligible for aid, (3) the equalized property valuation of a school district, (4) the state's guaranteed tax-base support per pupil, and (5) the total amount of state funding available for distribution. In many ways, these five factors are codependent. For example, the size of a school district's membership will obviously have a large effect on the school district's costs. Likewise, the total amount of state funding available will impact the amount of support per pupil the state can guarantee; the guarantee is set such that all available funds will be disbursed. It is the interrelations among the five variables that make Wisconsin's school funding laws so complex and make the fiscal impact of the choice program on public schools so difficult to determine.

MPCP Funding Mechanism 1990–98

For the first ten years of the choice program, the funding mechanism for the program was closely tied to MPS equalization aid. The per-pupil voucher amount equaled MPS equalization aid per pupil, and the total state payment to the voucher schools was deducted from the equalization aid payment to MPS. MPS was allowed to increase its tax levy, however, to offset this reduction in state aid.

MPCP Funding Mechanism 1999–Present

In the Wisconsin 1999–2001 biennial budget, the state legislature changed the MPCP funding mechanism. The per-pupil voucher amount no longer equals MPS equalization aid; instead, vouchers are equal to the previous year's voucher amount plus a statutory inflation-indexed increase. In addition, the total state payment to the voucher schools is no longer deducted solely from the MPS equalization aid payment: half of the total is deducted from MPS and the remaining half is deducted proportionately from each of the other 425 school districts' aid payments. All districts may increase their tax levies by the amount subtracted for MPCP from their equalization aid payments. As outlined in table 6.1, over the eleven years of the choice program, the state payments to voucher schools totaled $142.8 million.

Financial Impacts on Public Schools

"The financing of Milwaukee's choice program has, from the beginning, assumed that: (1) the state aid that MPS receives for each student should become portable and (2) if a choice parent picks a non-MPS school, aid that would have gone to MPS should follow that student to the choice school. These considerations are essential. It

Table 6.1. History of Voucher Payments

	MPCP Schools (N)	FTE Pupils* (N)	Voucher Amount Per Pupil	Total Voucher Payment
1990–91	7	300	$2,446	$733,800
1991–92	6	512	$2,643	$1,353,216
1992–93	11	594	$2,745	$1,630,530
1993–94	12	704	$2,985	$2,101,440
1994–95	12	771	$3,209	$2,474,139
1995–96	17	1288	$3,667	$4,723,096
1996–97	20	1616	$4,373	$7,066,768
1997–98	23	1497	$4,696	$7,029,912
1998–99	87	5803.5	$4,894	—$28,402,329
1999–00	91	7586.35	$5,106	$38,735,903
2000–01	103	9123.4	$5,326	$48,591,228
Total				$142,842,362

* All data from Wisconsin Legislative Fiscal Bureau except FTE (Full-Time Equivalent) for 1998–99, 1999–00, 2000–01 from Public Policy Forum.

is vital that the choice program sends a fiscal signal that gets the attention of MPS officials. If the program were modified to eliminate that, the fundamental goal of encouraging MPS to innovate and reform would be lost."
—Choice advocates Dr. Howard Fuller and George Mitchell (1999).

"MPS has had no competition because every year their budget goes up."
—Former Metropolitan Milwaukee Association of Commerce Chairman Robert O'Toole, *Milwaukee Sentinel* (February 18, 1995).

MPCP Funding Mechanism 1990–98

Until 1998–99, when the choice program expanded to include religious schools, the small number of children and schools participating in the program defused choice opponents' arguments that vouchers drained money from public schools. But after the exponential growth resulting from the inclusion of religious schools, many taxpayers, parents, and other concerned citizens began to wonder about the program's financial impact on public schools. As a result, several organizations and government agencies waded into the quagmire of Wisconsin's education funding laws and attempted to quantify the choice program's fiscal impacts on MPS. Not surprisingly, none of these groups reported the same findings, and each attempt to resolve the issue only raised more questions.

The various studies conducted during this time reported impacts on MPS in the 1998–99 school year ranging from a total loss of $28.7 million in state aid (Legislative Fiscal Bureau 1999) to a per-pupil gain in state aid of 2.6 percent (Fuller and Mitchell 1999). Other findings included a $22-million loss in state aid (Institute for Wisconsin's Future 1999), a $26.4-million loss in state aid (Toulmin 1999), and an unquantified "bubble" in the MPS revenue limit allowing for increased spending (Thompson 1998).

What appeared to be a simple question, "How much have vouchers cost Milwaukee's public schools?" did not have a simple answer. The state's convoluted school funding formulas, in conjunction with varying definitions of school costs and the limitations put on school districts' levying abilities, made deciphering the impact of choice a nearly futile exercise. Undeterred, the Public Policy Forum undertook its own analysis.[1]

We first attempted to calculate what the state aid to MPS would have been had there not been a choice program. It soon became apparent that this could not be resolved satisfactorily. First, there is no way to estimate how many voucher students would attend MPS if the choice program did not exist. For example, we cannot know how many four- and five-year-old kindergartners would have enrolled in MPS had the choice program not been an option. Adding another wrinkle is the Parents Advancing Values in Education (PAVE) scholarship program, which provided private scholarships to low-income religious school students until the choice program was expanded to religious schools. At that time, all PAVE scholarships were replaced with vouchers. It is unknown how many of the PAVE scholarship recipients were former MPS students or how many would become MPS students if the choice program ceased. Finally, when the program expanded in 1998 most of the new voucher recipients were already private school students. Many of them may have been receiving PAVE or other scholarships and some may have been paying tuition. Either way, we do not know how many would become MPS students were they no longer able to receive a voucher.

For simplicity's sake, we assumed that all voucher students would be MPS students had the program not existed. But even on this assumption we could not estimate with any certainty how MPS would be affected. This is because of factors two, four, and five of the equalization aid formula—MPS's costs, the state's guarantees, and the total amount of state funds available. Educating all these former voucher students would certainly have at least a marginal effect on MPS's costs, but because nothing other than grade level is known about these students, the actual effect cannot be estimated. MPS's costs vary by school, by degree of special education or bilingual services needed by a child, by grade level, and by many other factors. All we could say for certain is that the costs of running MPS would likely increase should the choice program cease.

But the largest unknowns, those causing the most uncertainty, are what the state's guarantee and statewide appropriation would have been had there not been a choice program. By reviewing legislative history and DPI budget requests, we found evidence that the existence of the choice program did, in fact, result in a greater statewide appropriation for K–12 funding and, therefore, in a different state guarantee than there would have been otherwise.[2] This is logical because the state appropriation was, in part, based on total statewide enrollment, which now included thousands of private school students in Milwaukee. Unfortunately, we could not know specifically what the differences in the appropriation or the guarantee would have been; thus we could not know specifically how much state aid MPS would have received had there not been a choice program. The only reason other organizations and agencies were able to estimate the fiscal impacts of choice on MPS in this way was that they assumed both the statewide appropriation and the statewide guarantee would have been the same whether or not there was a choice program in Milwaukee. Their results were therefore more speculative than empirical—as evidenced by the variance in their findings.

As the Public Policy Forum did not wish to add yet another guess about the impact on MPS to the debate, we attempted to change the nature of the inquiry. Instead of asking, What would MPS's state aid have been? we acknowledged that the addition of voucher recipients to the count of state-funded pupils increased the amount of aid appropriated for K–12 education and therefore asked, When the state aid pie grew because of choice, did the MPS slice of the pie grow?

We concluded that, because the voucher payment was equal to per-pupil MPS equalization aid, MPS aid had not been affected— the MPS slice of the pie grew proportionately with the growth of the pie as a whole. DPI calculated the total voucher payment simultaneously with MPS equalization aid. When this calculation was made, the MPS enrollment count included voucher students, artificially inflating the MPS equalization aid figure. If this "extra" aid were equal to the voucher payment, then the state aid retained by MPS was not affected by the subtraction of the voucher payment. However, if the voucher payment subtracted from MPS equalization aid were greater than the extra aid, then MPS lost aid to the choice program. We found that MPS had not lost state aid because the extra aid equaled the voucher payment (Public Policy Forum 1999).[3]

This finding implied that the state's education dollars were not following the child. Instead, there were simply more dollars to go around (and more children to educate as well). Unless the MPS size of the pie remained static, the dollars could not follow the child from his or her previous school to the voucher school. Put simply, parents' decisions did not have financial repercussions for the schools they left.

This finding was meaningful not only for MPS, but for public schools around the state as well. As the entire state aid pie grew, the choice program was having some sort of effect on districts outside Milwaukee. Because state aid was distributed via the equalization aid formula, the aid disbursed to one district affected the aid disbursed to every other district in the state. This fact conflicted with the choice program's enabling statute, section 119.23(5)(b), which required DPI to ensure the funding of the program did not negatively impact school districts other than Milwaukee. Partially in recognition of this conflict, and partially to mollify MPS supporters who saw the subtraction for the voucher payment as a loss in MPS aid, the 1999–2001 biennial state budget changed the funding mechanism for the voucher program.

MPCP Funding Mechanism 1999–Present

As explained above, starting with the 1999–2000 school year, the voucher payment is explicitly tied to the equalization aid of every district in the state. As a result, each Wisconsin school district receives an accounting statement detailing the amount of aid that is subtracted from its initial equalization aid figure to pay for the voucher payment, making the impact of the choice program on each district very clear.

Or is it? The Forum's analysis of this new funding scheme in its first year of use shows that not every school district experiences a real loss in aid, despite every district seeing a deduction for the voucher payment on its bottom line. We find that on average, school districts receive more total state aid and more state aid per pupil after the change in the funding mechanism than they had the year before. Overall, the average per-pupil difference in state aid from 1998–99 to 1999–2000 was a gain of $61 per pupil, adjusting for inflation, while the average total difference in state aid was a gain of $180,671 per district, adjusting for inflation.[4] MPS also enjoyed more aid, gaining $274 per pupil in state aid over the previous year (adjusted for inflation) (Public Policy Forum 2000).

The first year of changes in the choice program funding mechanism therefore did not result in less aid than the previous year for most districts. Is this a result of the funding scheme changes themselves? To find out, we compare the aid received in 1999–2000 under the new MPCP funding scheme to the aid that would have been received that year under the old scheme, using a simulated aid calculation provided by DPI. Excluding MPS for the moment, we find the average difference in per-pupil aid under the new laws was a loss of $21 per pupil (Public Policy Forum 2000).

This negligible difference between the two funding schemes leads us to conclude that the new funding mechanism is not, in all practicality, much different from the old one. Although the old laws required the voucher payment to be subtracted only from MPS equalization aid, obviously the statewide appropriation for equalization aid accounted for this voucher payment, affecting the aid of every district in the state. Until the funding scheme changed, however, this was never explicitly explained to the out-state school districts by the legislature, which is not to say that the legislature did not understand that the choice program potentially affected every school district's aid. Indeed, during the 1995 debates about expanding the program to include religious schools, Senator Chuck Chvala of Madison, as reported in a *Milwaukee Journal-Sentinel* article on May 13, 1995, warned other out-state legislators that according to legislative budget analysts, the increased costs could be "diverted not only from MPS, but all other districts that benefit from the school aid formula."

If altering the choice funding formula did not fundamentally change its impact on out-state districts, did it have an impact on MPS? We show in figure 6.1 that the change in the formula resulted in a gain of $102 per pupil for MPS over the old formula. More interestingly, we

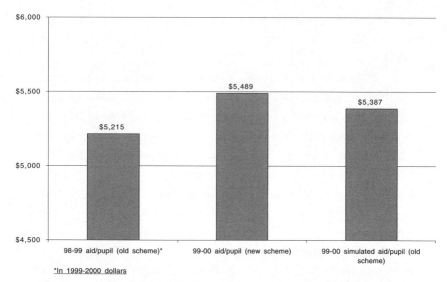

Figure 6.1. Milwaukee Public Schools General State Aid Per Pupil Under Old and New Milwaukee Parental Choice Program Funding Schemes

find that even if the choice funding formula had not changed, MPS would have received $172 more per pupil in state aid (adjusted for inflation) in 1999–2000 than in 1998–99, despite a 31 percent increase in the number of voucher students during that time period. For a program designed to spur radical improvement in MPS via competition, this finding is extraordinary. It shows that MPS was not being forced to compete with voucher schools for state dollars. Despite continued growth in the voucher program, MPS aid had also grown, most likely because the state aid pie grew at a faster rate than the voucher program.

Our results indicate that Wisconsin's choice funding laws are not designed so that the dollars follow the child. In fact, the state's education funding formulas are muting the effects of competition on MPS and the other Wisconsin districts. By not fully exposing school districts to either the positive or negative effects of competition, the funding laws financially insulate public school districts. Although this conclusion angers both advocates and opponents of choice, it is not an unexpected conclusion. Education policy researchers have found similar results in other states (Teske et al. 2000). In addition, as documented in a *Milwaukee Journal-Sentinel* report (July 26, 2000), some Wisconsin legislators acknowledge their intent was "never to use choice as [a] program that would cause financial hardship on school districts." Unfortunately, by not doing so, the choice funding laws become just another example of how marketlike competition is not living up to its promise. Parents are not able to hold schools accountable through financial mechanisms. Ultimately, as Fuller and Mitchell (1999) state, if districts are not exposed to market forces, they cannot be expected to respond to competition and improve their performance.

Now that the new funding mechanism has been in place for two school years, are our conclusions about its insulating properties holding true over time? By comparing the state aid received per pupil in 2000–01 with that received in 1999–2000, we find that the growth in state aid to MPS has slowed but has not yet had a negative fiscal effect on the district. After adjusting for inflation, MPS state aid per pupil is slightly lower in 2000–01, at $5,602.57 per pupil, than the year before, at $5,637.18 per pupil. Therefore, MPS aid has not grown but has merely kept pace with inflation. For the state as a whole, the second year of the new funding mechanism has seen 240 of 424 school districts[5] receiving more aid per pupil than the year before. On average, the state's school districts receive about $17 more per pupil in state aid than they did in 1999–2000, after adjusting for inflation; thus, the growth in the state aid pie as a whole has slowed to the rate of inflation.

In the end, the market theory explains little of the variation in state aid to schools. There is no clear relationship between the actions of voucher parents and the financial impacts on public schools. Wisconsin has created a funding scheme for choice that does not lead to clear winners and losers. The financial impacts on the only district that has lost students to choice, MPS, are at best ambiguous and at worst negligible. Districts across the state that are losing state aid because of the voucher program cannot compete directly with voucher schools located only in Milwaukee. The wrong school districts are being penalized. This has led these districts to complain that the costs of providing vouchers in Milwaukee are borne on their backs.

The Future of Choice Funding in Wisconsin

Such fiscal anxiety has led many out-state Wisconsin school districts to persuade their state legislators that the choice program is harming public education in their district. Many see statewide funding of a program limited to Milwaukee only as unfair, especially considering that Milwaukee already receives a greater share of state aid than its share of statewide public school enrollment would require—MPS enrolls 12 percent of the students in the state but receives 15 percent of all state aid.

As a result, several out-state legislators have become more vocal about the need to either change the funding mechanism yet again to be more fair to out-state taxpayers or to eliminate taxpayer-funded vouchers completely. Their calls culminated in the passage by the Democrat-controlled Wisconsin senate of a version of the 2001–03 state budget calling for the voucher amount to be cut in half, for the program to be funded separately from equalization aid to school districts, and for the capping of the number of voucher students at slightly more than ten thousand.[6] The perception, caused by the bookkeeping reduction of the voucher payment from districts' gross aid, is that Milwaukee's voucher program is draining money from public schools in Milwaukee and elsewhere. But the Legislative Fiscal Bureau and our own analysis both confirm that a district's change in aid has a stronger relationship to that district's property value than to the voucher payment.[7] In a true market, choices by Milwaukee parents should affect Milwaukee schools, while having little or no effect on schools in other areas of the state. Wisconsin's current choice funding scheme actually results in little impact on MPS, while giving out-state districts the perception that they are being penalized.

By muting the true effects of competition, Wisconsin's legislators have made meaningless the actions of parents in selecting a private school over a public school. This causes us to wonder: if the funding mechanism for the choice program cannot provide clear fiscal incentives or disincentives based on parents' actions, then why would any school feel a need to compete for the satisfaction of those parents? By insulating Milwaukee's public schools from the fiscal effects of competition, the Wisconsin choice program's statutory funding scheme is not meeting its "fundamental goal" of improving poor public schools. Indeed, in chapter 3 we found that public schools were not responding to nearby voucher schools as predicted. Perhaps this lack of clear financial incentives explains why public schools are not performing better when faced with voucher competition.

Financial Impacts on Private Schools

"Choice made it possible to open and maintain the school."
—Principal of secular school that joined MPCP in 1995.

"When the school joined the choice program, it was like our dreams were coming true."
—Principal of parochial school that joined MPCP in 1998.

"If the choice program were removed, the school would be closed."
—Principal of secular school that joined MPCP in 1998.

The choice program has obviously had a tremendous financial impact on most of the participating private schools. It has facilitated the opening of several brand new schools, ensured the continued existence of some financially distressed schools, and strengthened the fiscal health of nearly every other participating school. For example, according to a *Milwaukee Sentinel* story (February 17, 1994), after the Milwaukee archdiocese announced it would be closing St. Leo School because of financial problems, State Rep. Annette "Polly" Williams and Mayor John Norquist announced from the steps of the school the proposed expansion of the choice program to include religious schools. The money made available to private schools through the choice program has become so essential to many of the voucher schools that according to a *Milwaukee Journal-Sentinel* report on June 16, 2001, threatened cuts in the statutory voucher amount sparked a prayer vigil by principals and parents in the Wisconsin state capitol rotunda.

The exact effect of voucher funds on each school, however, is difficult to gauge without detailed financial information on individual school and church revenue and costs. Some data give us an idea of the magnitude of this effect. The DPI has information on per-pupil expenditures of participating schools. Other public data sources include county court records and newspaper accounts. In addition, in the fall of 1999 the Public Policy Forum conducted face-to-face interviews with the administrators of 17 choice schools. The interviews lasted between thirty and sixty minutes and consisted of twelve open-ended questions. Several of the questions focus on the financial importance of the choice program to the participating school.

The administrative interviews represent approximately 20 percent of the schools participating in the choice program in 1999–2000. The schools are characteristic of all the schools in the choice program (table 6.2). Ten of the sample schools are religious schools, compared with 70 percent in the entire program. The average enrollment of the sample schools is 113, which is somewhat smaller that the program average of 195. Most schools in the sample opened in the 1990s, although 4 have been in operation for over fifty years, which mirrors all participating schools. The choice schools represented in the interviews are rela-

Table 6.2. Characteristics of Sampled Schools vs. Population of MPCP Schools

Religion	Location	Size	Year Opened	Years in MPCP	Grades Served	Percent Voucher
		Characteristics of MPCP Schools*				
70% are religious	28 on Southside, 41 on Northside, 13 on Westside, 4 on Eastside	Average 195 students	Range from 1857 to 1999	Average 1.8 years	73% of all students in K5–8	Average 51%
		Characteristics of Schools Participating in Interviews				
No	W	29	1998	2	K4–8	100
No	W	62	1996	1	K3–3	36
Christian Nondenominational	N	47	1998	1	K4–3	32
Lutheran	NE	132	1891	1	K4–8	96
No	W	43	1979	3	K4–3	60
Lutheran	NE	111	1919	1	K4–8	80
No	E	28	1972	9	K4–K5	32
No	W	110	1998	1	K4–6	100
Lutheran	NW	47	1993	1	K4–6	38
Catholic	S	62	1996	1	5–8	73
Catholic	N	188	1953	2	K4–8	17
Catholic	S		1999	1	K4–8	30
Christian Nondenominational	NW	32	1970	2	K4–K5	70
Catholic	S	332	1872	1	K4–8	78
Catholic	W	235	1908	2	K4–8	83
No	NW	107	1996	4	K4–7	60
No	E	239	1995	4	K4–8	96

* Data are from the 1998–99 school year and represent the total population of 86 schools.

tively new participants in the program, which compares to the overall length of program participation at the time of 1.8 years. All the schools in the sample are elementary or K–8 schools, as are most of the participating schools. In the sample schools the percentage of voucher students in the total student body ranges from 30 to 100 percent, with an average of 64 percent. The overall average percentage of voucher students is 51 percent.

According to our interviews with voucher school administrators, the majority of the schools (9 of the 17) joined the choice program for financial reasons. As put succinctly by one administrator, "The school became involved in choice to survive financially. Tuition costs were more than most people could afford and it was difficult to send their children to the school." As stated by another administrator, "The school wanted to remain a neighborhood school, but people in the neighborhood cannot afford tuition." Four administrators volunteered that without the choice program their schools would have to close down.[8]

By looking at the percentage of the student body receiving vouchers, we can better understand vouchers' role in the revenue of a school. Choice schools report a total enrollment in 2000–01 of 20,290 students. Approximately half of these students are voucher recipients. The other students pay tuition, receive private scholarships, or, in some cases, are MPS students who attend "partnership schools" and do not pay tuition via contract with MPS.[9] Sixty of the 103 schools participating in the voucher program in 2000–01 have enrollments in which at least 50 percent of the student body is receiving a voucher. Thirteen of these schools have enrollments of 90 percent or more voucher students; 6 enroll only voucher students. Eleven schools have fewer than 10 percent voucher students. Therefore, in half of all voucher schools, less than half of the families served pay tuition.

As a result, voucher money makes up a high percentage of the revenue of many choice schools. Using expenditure data from 1998–99,

Table 6.3. Voucher Payment as a Percentage of Total Estimated
Revenues, 1998–99

Voucher Payment as Percent of Estimated Revenue	MPCP Schools (N)
100	5
80–99	15
60–79	15
40–59	12
20–39	16
<19	16
Total	79

the most recent year of complete information, we estimate the percent of a school's revenue that comes from vouchers. A school's total revenue is estimated by aggregating per-pupil expenditures. A school's voucher payment is calculated by multiplying the number of voucher recipients by the per-pupil voucher amount. On average, the voucher payment represents 50 percent of the estimated total revenue of the 79 private schools reporting expenditure data. The voucher payment equals the total estimated revenue for 5 of these schools. An additional 30 schools receive more than 60 percent of their estimated revenue from vouchers. Just 23 of the 79 reporting schools receive less than 25 percent of their estimated revenue from vouchers (table 6.3). The magnitude of the schools' reliance on the voucher payment was illustrated when the Wisconsin State Senate voted to decrease the per-pupil voucher amount in June 2001. A letter sent to the state senate leadership by voucher supporters argued that without the voucher program, 44 of the 103 participating voucher schools would be forced to close.

A second impact of voucher income is how it affects a participating school's ability to collect revenue. Voucher payments are sent to each school four times a year by checks made out to the parents. The parent must restrictively endorse the check to the school. Judging from our conversations with voucher school administrators, however, it appears that many schools avoid the potential delays this requirement might cause by having parents sign a form at the beginning of the year allowing the school to endorse the checks for them. School administrators report that collecting four reliable voucher payments from the state each year is far easier than collecting tuition from each family throughout the year. Schools know the dates these payments will be received and, based on voucher student enrollment, the amount of each payment. This reliability can even allow schools to work out alternative methods for tuition payments—schools, knowing when and how much voucher revenue will be available, may be more flexible or lenient with parents who need extra time or consideration when making tuition payments. In our interviews, 13 of 17 administrators feel the choice program has benefited the tuition-paying parents in the school, either by allowing those who could no longer afford tuition to continue at the school or by relieving some of the burden on the other parents. The schools that are most able to relieve this burden are the schools with low per-pupil costs. Schools with per-pupil costs lower than the voucher amount can use the voucher revenue to offset the expense of educating the rest of their student body. Table 6.4 illustrates this point. Of the 79 schools reporting 1998–99 financial data, in 13 the ratio of voucher revenue to total revenue is greater than the ratio of voucher students to total students, meaning they are able to use voucher income to subsidize their other students.[10] On the other hand, 16 schools must subsidize the costs of educating voucher students with other income because their per-pupil costs are greater than the voucher amount.

In some cases, we find that voucher revenue can alleviate a participating school's dependency on tuition to such an extent that the school may choose to expend less effort collecting unpaid tuition. Using Milwaukee County Circuit Court records, we find 15 voucher schools listed as plaintiffs in civil or small claims cases seeking money judgments against individuals. These are likely to be cases involving unpaid tuition. A sample of 4 of these schools shows that, in some instances, the frequency of the filings declined after a school joined the choice program. For example, the school that has filed the most of these types of claims, a Catholic high school, averaged twenty-one claims per year in civil or small claims court between 1985 and 1997. In the following four years, while participating in the choice program, the school has filed a total of thirty-eight claims, or an average of ten per year. The other 3 schools had less dramatic, but similar, patterns. Voucher income appears to have improved these schools' financial outlooks from a tuition-collection point of view.

But after a review of all the financial information it should come as no surprise that, according to administrators, the greatest effect that choice has on participating schools is to increase the schools' total revenue. Several of the administrators interviewed, when asked how the choice program has changed their school, replied that the program has allowed their schools to spend more in certain areas. Six administrators specifically mention increasing teachers' salaries and five administrators mention hiring more teachers and specialists such as social workers and child psychologists. "[The choice program] allows teachers to be paid well here. It is not easy to compete with public schools in terms of having good teachers," explains one administrator from a Christian elementary school. The principal of an archdiocesan school elaborates, "[The program] has broadened the availability of resources and good teaching for kids. As an administrator, the program has allowed me to pay the teachers a just wage . . . and reduces the turnover rate in teachers. If we couldn't provide a good wage, then we couldn't keep the teachers." Another Catholic school principal states that voucher revenue has funded four new teachers and raised the salaries of the veteran teachers by five thousand dollars.

In addition, four administrators credit the choice program with allowing them to provide better learning resources such as textbooks and computers. "We used to use old textbooks donated by the Archdiocese. Now we can buy all the necessary resources," says the administrator

Table 6.4. Voucher Enrollment and Revenue

	Voucher Payment as Percent of Total Estimated Revenue*	Voucher Enrollment as Percent of Total Enrollment	Difference Between Percent Revenue and Percent Enrollment
Louis Tucker Academy	128	100	−28
St. John Kanty School	57	36	−21
Catholic East Elementary School	70	50	−19
Gospel Lutheran School	88	71	−17
Medgar Evers Academy	79	63	−16
St. Anthony's School	80	67	−13
Our Lady of Sorrows School	47	36	−11
Resurrection Catholic Academy	69	61	−8
St. Josaphat Parish School	60	53	−7
Texas Bufkin Academy	102	95	−7
St. Peter Immanuel Lutheran School	25	18	−7
Our Lady Queen of Peace Parish	27	20	−6
Oklahoma Avenue Lutheran School	24	18	−6

School			
St. Leo Catholic Urban Academy	78	83	5
Blyden Delany Academy	95	100	5
St. Rose Catholic Academy	79	84	5
Marva Collins Preparatory School	81	87	6
St. Matthew	37	47	11
Ceria M. Travis Academy	80	92	11
Sherman Park Preschool	60	71	11
Milwaukee Multicultural Academy	89	100	11
Yeshiva Elementary School	32	44	12
Community Vision Academy	46	59	13
Lutheran Special School	22	35	13
Urban Day School	74	88	13
Parklawn Christian School	19	33	15
Harambee Community School	51	70	19
Notre Dame Middle School	48	73	25
Gray's Child Development Center	48	85	36

* Where voucher payment surpasses estimated revenue, the overpayment must be returned to DPI.
Note: Only includes schools where percent estimated revenue is + or − 5 percent of percent enrollment.

of a parochial school. Two administrators demonstrate the choice program's impact by pointing out improvements to the learning environment, for example, new desks and bookshelves. One administrator explains that the school's after-school enrichment program is funded by the voucher payment. "More enrichment programs are being offered in the arts, youth choir, and drama club" at this Catholic K–8 school.

The choice program revenue also supports capital improvements, in some instances necessary maintenance issues such as fixing a leaky roof. Other improvements include the building of expansions and renovations. A cursory search of building permit records shows that since joining the program, voucher schools have requested permits for building projects estimated to cost a total of $14.1 million.[11] Of these permits, most were designated as alterations; the twenty-seven permits totaled $2,928,326 in estimated costs. There were six permits obtained for building additions, which totaled $9,810,132 in estimated costs.[12] Although the permits themselves do not indicate whether the work was ever completed or what the actual costs were, visual observations of the schools show marked changes in many of the schools that obtained permits for additions or alterations.

Judging from our interviews, it seems most participating schools are benefiting financially from the choice program. A major principle of parent-driven accountability is that schools will either flourish or fail based on the actions of parents and the dollars they bring to their school of choice. If no voucher schools appear to be losing money, how then does the market system successfully provide accountability in Milwaukee? The reality is that it does not. The Milwaukee choice program does not operate as a free market, but rather as a government subsidy. A free market implies that suppliers will respond to consumer demand. If demand is higher than supply, the price of the good can be increased. This cannot happen with the voucher provided to a parent in Milwaukee. The result is a disincentive for schools to operate efficiently.

Because the choice program is designed to pay a private school's actual cost per pupil or the statutory voucher amount, whichever is less, schools that spend less than the voucher amount must pay the difference back to the state.[13] A free market implies that suppliers will attempt to optimize efficiency to maximize profits, but a voucher school cannot maximize profits—it must maximize spending, instead. In 1999–2000, 37 of the 82 participating schools owed a total of $1,196,544 to the state because their 1998–99 school year costs per pupil were less than the voucher amount (table 6.5).[14]

Most schools avoid making any repayment to the state by ensuring their actual costs meet or exceed the voucher amount. Although little data are available regarding private schools' costs, we do know through such evidence as that illustrated above that voucher schools are spending more than they did before joining the program. Because choice proponents have long touted private schools as a good investment for taxpayers because these schools are able to do more with less money, this incentive to spend more seems to be illogical—a funding mechanism argued to spur competition actually ends up promoting inefficiency in what were previously promoted as efficient schools.

The result of a market approach to education should be that good schools succeed and poor schools close. Yet the voucher program makes it possible for a school that is unable to attract enough tuition-paying students to continue operation by opening its door to voucher students. What has happened, in economics terms, is that voucher schools have acted as "rent-seekers," obtaining a transfer of wealth from the government instead of competing for wealth in an open market (Adler 1996). The "rents" sought are returns that are greater than those a competitive marketplace would allow, or, in other words, the difference between the per-pupil voucher amount and a school's tuition. In 2000 this difference was estimated to be a total of $11 million across all the voucher schools (Egen, Holmes, and Mincberg 2000; Nelson, Egen, and Holmes 2001; People for the American Way 2002). Thus, it is very diffi-

Table 6.5. MPCP School Cost Per Pupil, 1998–99 (Voucher Amount
Was $4,894)

	Cost Per Pupil	School Owed DPI
St. Anthony's School	$4,084	$123,807
Catholic East Elementary School	$3,537	$107,852
Salam School	$3,858	$95,423
St. John Kanty School	$3,096	$93,047
Resurrection Catholic Academy	$4,298	$82,864
Our Lady of Sorrows School	$3,792	$67,338
Gospel Lutheran School	$3,957	$61,045
St. Peter Immanuel Lutheran School	$3,565	$56,694
Our Lady Queen of Peace Parish	$3,733	$51,917
St. Josaphat Parish School	$4,321	$45,816
St. Margaret Mary School	$3,792	$44,356
St. Sebastian School	$4,144	$42,750
Mother of Good Counsel School	$4,383	$41,646
St. Bernadette School	$3,891	$38,682
Woodson Academy	$4,794	$31,943
Louis Tucker Academy	$3,835	$26,090
Corpus Christi School	$4,484	$25,223
Medgar Evers Academy	$3,906	$24,335
St. Paul Catholic School	$3,457	$17,244
Blessed Sacrament School	$3,789	$17,121
Holy Redeemer Christian Academy	$4,841	$15,390
St. Alexander School	$4,218	$12,506
Oklahoma Avenue Lutheran School	$3,725	$10,832
Mt. Calvary Lutheran School	$4,741	$10,407
Our Lady of Good Hope School	$4,694	$8,260
Early View Academy of Excellence	$4,845	$7,895
Blyden Delany Academy*	$5,132	$7,358
St. Vincent Pallotti School	$4,694	$6,688
Family Academy Inc.*	$5,036	$5,874
St. Helen Grade School	$4,654	$4,633
Urban Day School*	$5,754	$3,672
North Milwaukee Christian School*	$7,375	$2,447
Nazareth Lutheran School	$4,622	$1,907
Marva Collins Preparatory School*	$5,262	$1,225
Yeshiva Elementary School*	$6,700	$1,223
St. Leo Catholic Urban Academy*	$5,177	$614
St. Veronica School	$4,859	$420

Source: Wisconsin Department of Public Instruction

* For schools with costs greater than the voucher amount, the difference owed to DPI is
due to audited enrollment figures.

cult to use free-market theories to evaluate a program that is clearly operating not on free-market principles but as a government subsidy. That schools on a path to closure can remain open by deciding to take taxpayer-funded vouchers in lieu of tuition thwarts the idea that only good schools thrive in the education market.

Conclusion

Voucher programs are designed to improve education by allowing private schools to compete with public schools for taxpayer dollars. When a program is designed so that the dollars follow the child, clear winners and losers should emerge. The result is that parents' actions in selecting one school over another should have a clear fiscal impact on both the gaining and losing schools, spurring the losing schools to improve. In this way, the design of a voucher program's finance mechanism can provide another layer of accountability.

We test this third prong of accountability with an extensive analysis of how the system works in Milwaukee. For public schools, it is undeniable that Wisconsin's funding formula for vouchers was designed to mute the possible competitive effects of gaining or losing voucher students. Despite the fact that the education funding pie in Wisconsin has grown, the voucher funding mechanism and its bottom-line reduction in state aid lead districts that are hundreds of miles away from any voucher competition to feel they are losing money to voucher schools. Meanwhile, the financial impact on the only public school district that directly competes with voucher schools has been negligible.

While the choice program's impact on public schools remains murky, voucher income has certainly had a positive financial impact on participating private schools. Private school revenue is enhanced by the voucher payments, which also reduce the uncertainty that can arise when relying on tuition. Yet the financial effect of parents choosing private voucher schools does not allow the identification of either winning or losing schools. The Milwaukee choice program does not operate as a true market. Schools that are in high demand by voucher parents cannot raise the price of their admission, and schools on the verge of closing owing to the lack of demand from tuition-paying parents are able to continue operating by relying on voucher parents, who, as we discussed in the previous chapter, are forced to make schooling decisions with inadequate information.

The financial system at work in Milwaukee is incapable of ensuring that schools compete for education dollars. What should be a simple formula—the dollars follow the child—is not. The complexity of the funding formula results in schools having no real way of measuring the financial impact of parents' choices. Thus competition is muted and neither public nor private schools are forced to respond to market forces. There should be no expectation, therefore, that these schools will have any incentive to compete by improving their performance. This is a design flaw, to be sure, but it need not be fatal. Policymakers have the ability to create accountable voucher programs in which schools truly do compete for education dollars.

CHAPTER SEVEN

Choice School Accountability

A Consensus of Views

I n the previous chapters of this book, we presented systematic evidence that the competitive theory of accountability for private choice schools is not working in the real world of Milwaukee. Milwaukee's choice program is not structured to induce either voucher schools or public schools to respond to parents' demands; parents struggle to communicate their desires to these schools because they lack the needed information to make informed schooling decisions; and the state legislature has insulated schools from the financial effects of competition, further diminishing parents in their attempt to hold schools accountable. Unfortunately, when parents' decisions lack weight, schools have little incentive to improve. The result is that school choice fails to live up to its promise of bettering education in all schools.

Our findings do not mean, however, that school choice is doomed. Rather, we argue that for school choice to be effective as an educational reform, parents should not be considered the only means for keeping the system accountable. Parents need support from some kind of outside accountability mechanism. This argument is controversial. As noted in chapter 1, some proponents of school choice believe accountability standards for voucher schools will lead to significant state intrusion into private school operations and are just another political device for eventually eliminating school choice (Mitchell 1996: 11). Other proponents argue that one cannot find a more regulated system than the public schools, and yet this regulation has no correlation with student achievement (statements made at Wisconsin Assembly Hearing of the Committee on Urban Education, February 28, 1996). On the other hand, those wary of school choice as public policy argue that public funds should not be spent on a program with limited oversight.

Is there a middle ground between the view that voucher schools should operate completely free of regulations and the view that they should operate under similar oversight as public schools? We looked for a consensus on this controversial issue by constructing an accountability framework based on the three necessary components: first, how parents can best send schools clear messages about their needs; second, how schools can best respond to parents' actions; and finally, how the resulting financial consequences can best encourage schools to improve.

Methodology

To find consensus on a method of holding voucher schools accountable to parents and the children that attend them and to the public that supports them, we assembled a national panel of academic researchers to help design a research method and analyze the results.[1] Given the politically volatile nature of school choice policy, the academic panel felt it critical to include individuals directly or indirectly involved in choice schools as an integral part of the study. Our panel therefore created a research design that focused first on the concerns of school stakeholders. This stakeholder approach is distinguished from other types of research because the key findings are the result of testing hypotheses developed by individuals who are affected by a school choice program, rather than exclusively by members of the academic community or a legislative body (see Worthen and Sanders 1987 for a discussion of this method). The panel believed that if individuals affected by the development of school choice accountability are included in the process, the probability of establishing a widely accepted process is increased. Indeed, previous research has shown that if stakeholder groups are included in the development of standards, there is a better chance the standards will be perceived as unbiased (Oakes 1986).

In choosing the stakeholders we asked ourselves the following question: Who will be most affected by the criteria and variables that will be used in establishing school choice accountability? In answering this question, we viewed the inclusion of the following groups, representing both public and voucher schools, as imperative. The first group of stakeholders includes school administrators, parents, students, and teachers.[2] These stakeholders have extensive knowledge about the issues surrounding school choice accountability and a vested interest in the outcomes of this study. In this chapter, we refer to this set of stakeholders as school-based stakeholders. The inclusion of stakeholders from the broader community is also important. The second group includes taxpayers because taxpayer money is being used to fund this form of school choice.[3]

To establish the broadest consensus possible, we gathered data from both Milwaukee and Cleveland. We include Cleveland because it is the only other city in the country to offer low-income students a chance to attend private school with public funds (although the money provided to parents is called a scholarship rather than a voucher). The Cleveland private school choice program began in the fall of 1996. Participating children in Cleveland can attend either public or private, sectarian or nonsectarian schools. Scholarships are offered to students in kindergarten through eighth grade. The scholarship is worth either 75 or 90 percent of tuition, depending on family income, with a maximum value of $2,250. Seventy-five percent of choice recipients must be from families at or below 100 percent of the federal poverty level. Another 25 percent are chosen from those families with incomes between 100 and

200 percent of federal poverty standards. A lottery drawing is held for eligible applicants. In the program's first year of operation, 1,800 students were recipients of scholarships and enrolled at 51 participating choice schools. The majority of these schools were sectarian. Twenty percent of these students had attended a private school in the previous year. In the 2000–01 school year, 3,000 Cleveland children attended 50 private religious or nonsectarian schools.

The first phase of our research design was to interview school-based stakeholders in the two cities about their needs with respect to school accountability. We conducted one-on-one, face-to-face interviews with 270 administrators, teachers, and parents in the spring of 1997. The interviews focused on the following issues: what kinds of information should be available for holding schools accountable? what is the best means for determining the validity of the information? what kind of criteria, if any, should voucher schools adhere to? and finally, what consequences should there be for schools that fail to adhere to these guidelines?

We targeted our interviews with school-based stakeholders by first choosing 5 public and 5 private choice schools each in Cleveland and Milwaukee. The chosen schools were representative of the racial, economic, and geographic diversity of the two cities.[4] We next conducted interviews with the administrators of these schools and with teachers and parents who were affiliated with the schools. Therefore, the majority of our interviews were with individuals affiliated with one of these 20 public and private choice schools in Cleveland and Milwaukee.[5] In addition, the majority of our interviews were conducted with people affiliated with primary school education. But we did conduct interviews with individuals affiliated with 3 high schools. We included fewer high schools because school choice, as it has developed in Cleveland and Milwaukee, has largely focused on elementary school children.[6]

We asked interviewees a series of fourteen open-ended and one

Table 7.1. Number of Interviews of School-Based Respondents

	All	Cleveland Private Choice School	Milwaukee Private Choice School	Cleveland Public School	Milwaukee Public School
Parent	153	34	40	35	44
School administrator	25	7	7	5	6
Teacher	92	22	22	26	22
Total	270	63	69	66	72

closed-ended question. The questions were written for parents but were rephrased for teachers and administrators, who were asked their percep-tion of what information parents want to know about a school. The interviews ranged in time from ten minutes to one hour and ten min-utes, averaging thirty minutes. Table 7.1 illustrates the number of com-pleted interviews by school-based stakeholders.

The second phase of research was a telephone survey of taxpay-ers in Ohio and Wisconsin conducted in fall 1997. The survey questions were based on our findings from the interviews with school-based stake-holders. We analyzed and categorized the open-ended interview data from the school-based stakeholders, which basically called for grouping the hundreds of responses into a manageable number of categories cap-turing all of the variations in the responses.[7] We used these responses to create a closed-ended survey. The resulting survey was administered by telephone to a random sample of 771 taxpayers in Ohio and Wiscon-sin.[8] Table 7.2 illustrates the percentage distribution of surveyed respon-dents compared to the population in Ohio and Wisconsin. The sample population is representative of the estimated population in all cases ex-cept for African Americans in Wisconsin. For this reason, we ran the subsequent analyses by weighting the African Americans in Wisconsin to represent the population.[9]

Table 7.2. Percentage Distribution of Sampled Taxpayers and of the
Adult Population in Ohio and Wisconsin on Selected Social
Characteristics

Characteristic	Ohio Sample	Ohio Population	Wisconsin Sample	Wisconsin Population
Adult population, age 35 and above*	65%	62%	67%	63%
Gender, female	55%	52%	53%	51%
Ethnicity, African American	12%	11%	12%	5%
Median household income	$39,000	$36,000	$39,000	$38,000
Education, one or more years of college	30%	22%	28%	16%

* The population estimates represent the latest available estimates from the 1990 census
general population survey.

Findings: Support for Vouchers

Before discussing the specific interview and survey findings as
they relate to accountability, it is instructive to examine overall public
support in Ohio and Wisconsin for school choice. Our school-based
stakeholders were not specifically asked about their support or opposition to school choice in our interviews. Informally, however, many individuals expressed their opinion regarding school choice. The majority
favored school choice. Our telephone survey of taxpayers more accurately quantified public support. As table 7.3 illustrates, a great majority
of taxpayers in Ohio and Wisconsin supported school choice. Seventy-
six percent of those surveyed supported school choice. This number
represents the sum of those who supported this program for low-income
parents only and those who supported this program for any child regardless of their parents' income. The percentage agreeing with these
statements were 23 percent and 53 percent, respectively. Eighty-three
percent believed that religious schools should be allowed to participate
in a choice program. In addition, 77 percent of those surveyed in Ohio

Table 7.3. Percentage of Taxpayers Who Agree with Following Statements by Respondent Characteristics

		Race/Ethnicity		Income		
Statements	Total	White	African American	Low <$25,000	Middle $26,000–$60,000	High >$60,000
I *favor* providing tax money to parents only under the condition that the tax money is provided to low-income parents.	23	23	28	25	23	23
I *favor* providing tax money to parents for any child regardless of their parents' income.	53	52	61	54	55	49
I *oppose* providing tax money to parents to allow their children to attend private schools.	22	23	11	19	21	26
Religious schools *should be* allowed to participate in a choice program.	83	84	91	88	81	85
Choice programs *should be* expanded to include all school districts in the state.	76	75	82	78	80	64
N	771	631	95	184	369	121

and 74 percent in Wisconsin believed the current school choice programs should be expanded to include all school districts in the state.
The average across both states was 76 percent.

We also report support for choice by race and income of the
survey respondent. Our survey indicates that African American taxpayers were more likely to support vouchers, at 89 percent versus 75 percent
for white taxpayers. These findings are consistent with a poll by the Joint
Center for Political and Economic Studies (1997). This survey found that
almost 87 percent of African Americans aged twenty-six to thirty-five
supported school choice. The findings also indicate that regardless of
income there was generally high support for school vouchers. Our
higher income respondents, those households earning greater than
$60,000 per year, were somewhat more likely to be opposed to vouchers,
at 26 percent compared to 21 percent for our middle-income group and
19 percent for our lower-income group. Moreover, support for a
voucher for families regardless of income is a bit lower among our highest income group. This is somewhat inconsistent with recently published
work by Terry Moe, who found that there was clearly a class dimension
to support of a universal voucher, or a voucher that is available to all
parents regardless of income, in his analysis of a 1995 nationwide school
choice survey. The higher a respondent's income, the more inclined he
or she was to support universal school vouchers (2001: 330).

Parents' Informational Needs

Before exploring the individual criteria that our school-based
stakeholders felt were important for accountability, it is important to
point out their overwhelming desire that very little information be kept
private. In the interviews, we specifically asked our stakeholders, "Are
there any kinds of information you think a school should be able to
keep private?" Since *private* can be defined in many ways, our interviewers defined the word to mean any information that would not be re-

leased to the public. Three out of four school-based stakeholders indicated that nothing should be kept private except for individual student
records. Summed up by one parent, "Personal family information
should be kept private. Everything else should be open to the public."
An interviewer of a private school teacher summed up that teacher's
response in this manner: "At first when I asked this question the teacher
said a big, 'No!' And when I asked her why she was so emphatic, she
said anything a school is hiding makes her wonder what is going on.
Then she said as far as a student's personal background, economics, etc.
. . . that should be kept between the parent and that specific teacher."
These statements were echoed by a majority of respondents. Our findings are consistent with those reported by Moe in his in-depth analysis
of a 1995 survey of public support for school choice (2001). As Moe
writes, "By huge majorities, Americans think private schools should be
subject to basic regulations—for curriculum, teacher qualifications, financial audits, student testing—that hold them accountable for quality
and proper management" (2001: 341).

Now we turn to the focus of the interviews: what information
school-based stakeholders believe is important for parents to have in
order to hold schools accountable. Specifically we asked parents, "What
would you want to know about schools in order to make a decision
about where to send your own children?" The question was reworded
for teachers and administrators so as to refer not to their own children
but to the children that may attend their schools.

On specific criteria there is fundamental agreement among
school-based stakeholders of both public and private schools on the
information parents need to make a decision and, thus, to hold a school
accountable. Table 7.4 lists the major criteria. Information on the
school's program, primarily its curriculum and method of instruction,
is the piece of necessary information most commonly mentioned in our
interviews. This is true across all three stakeholder groups: parents,
teachers, and administrators. A private voucher school parent in Cleve-

Table 7.4. Criteria Recommended by School-Based Stakeholders
in Cleveland and Milwaukee

	Parents (N = 153) (%)	Teachers (N = 92) (%)	School Administrators (N = 25) (%)
School program	59	67	60
Teachers	45	45	24
Outcomes general	35	39	60
Outcomes test scores	15	12	40
School characteristics	31	30	44
Safety and discipline	28	35	28
Reputation of school	9	20	28
Parent involvement	12	18	8

Note: The total percentage in each column exceeds 100 percent because respondents on average mentioned between two and three criteria.

land summed up the responses of a number of parents this way: "I would want to know the teacher-student ratio, if they have computer instruction, and their curriculum. I want to know if the school teaches foreign language in the early grades." Information on teachers is the next most common response by both parents and teachers. A public school teacher in Milwaukee characterizes this type of response in saying, "Parents want to know that teachers are qualified, if they are certified, and what kind of experience and experiences they have."

School administrators stated that general school outcomes—for example, the percentage of students advancing to the next grade level—school characteristics—for example, class size and makeup of student body—and test scores are more important than teacher qualifications in making a decision about a school and holding a school accountable. For parents too, general outcomes were an important piece of information, but less so than teacher qualifications. Fifteen percent of parents believed information on test scores is important compared to 40 percent of administrators. All groups agreed that information on safety and discipline of the school is important for holding a school accountable. Yet this was felt to be less important than information on the school's program or general school outcomes. Much less important for parents was the reputation of the school.

Ensuring Schools Respond to Parents' Desires

Making information available to parents is the first step in helping them to make informed choices. How to gather and disseminate this information is a critical second step. We asked our school-based stakeholders a closed-ended question about who should gather the requested information on schools, make sure that the information is accurate, and disseminate it to parents. The options included the state department of education, private schools themselves, an accreditation agency, a privately run parent information center, or no agency needs to be responsible, parents will decide for themselves. Table 7.5 lists the percent of respondents who agreed or disagreed with an option.

Interestingly, our interviews uncovered consistently low support among the school-based stakeholders for having parents gather in-

Table 7.5. Percentage of School-Based Stakeholders Selecting Agree or Disagree to Question: "Who Should Be Responsible for Gathering Information about Private Schools?"

	Agree	Disagree
Privately run parent information center is created to collect and distribute information about schools	64	36
The state department of education	62	38
The private schools themselves	54	46
Schools are accredited through a private accreditation agency	50	50
No agency needs to be responsible; parents will decide for themselves	9	91

Note: $N = 268$. There were 49 missing cases for this question.

formation on their own. Less than 9 percent of stakeholders agreed that parents should be left alone with this responsibility. The two entities receiving the greatest level of support were a privately run parent information center and the state department of education. Private schools themselves and an accreditation agency received support from 54 percent and 50 percent of the stakeholders, respectively. Our stakeholders were also given the opportunity to comment on the choices given. What these comments revealed was a desire that other options should be included in the list. Several administrators at private schools felt that any information-collecting entity must include representation from private schools. As one administrator of a private voucher school stated, "A state agency is too bureaucratic, I definitely disagree with that option."

The Perspective of Taxpayers

The next step in the study, the taxpayer survey, tested whether there was widespread acceptance of the information deemed important by the school-based stakeholders in the face-to-face interviews. To test general public support for mandating the reporting of this information, in our telephone survey we presented taxpayers with a list of possible items that voucher schools could be required to release to the public. Specifically, we asked the following question (rephrased for residents of Ohio): "In Wisconsin, some low-income parents receive money to pay tuition at private schools. These private schools are called choice schools. I will read a list of things that choice schools might be asked to report to the public. Please tell me whether you as a taxpayer think each item should be voluntary or mandatory for a private choice school to report the information to the public. Do you feel it should be voluntary or mandatory for private choice schools to report (Read item below) to the public?"[10]

What follows in this chapter is a discussion of our findings, combining what our taxpayer survey data show with what we previously learned from our school-based stakeholder interviews. We acknowledge it is important to be cautious when comparing the responses by school-based stakeholders to the responses of taxpayers. This is because some of the apparent differences may be explained by the two methods used. School-based stakeholders were participating in face-to-face, primarily open-ended interviews in which they were asked what kind of information they need to hold a school accountable, how this information should be collected, and what consequences, if any, schools should experience if they withhold this information. Taxpayers, on the other hand, were participating in telephone interviews in which the questions were closed-ended. Moreover, the questions asked of taxpayers were a direct outcome of the responses given by the school-based stakeholders. In this way the taxpayers were testing whether broad support existed for the accountability criteria developed by the stakeholders. The different formats mean that direct comparisons of responses must be treated with care. Nonetheless, because of the need to be sensitive to all opinions in the creation of accountability guidelines, we believe it is essential to highlight both similarities and differences in the responses of the two groups of respondents.

We found from our school-based stakeholder interviews that information on school programs and teachers is most important for parents. Given this value, it is no surprise to find that, as reported in table 7.6, 73 percent of the taxpayers surveyed felt reporting of school curriculum and 66 percent felt reporting of methods of teaching should be mandatory. We also found consistency with the school-based stakeholders when we asked taxpayers about information on the qualifications of teachers and administrators: 85 percent of the surveyed taxpayers believed this information should be mandatory.

For parents, the three most important items of information needed when making a decision on where to send their children were curriculum, teachers, and general student outcomes. Taxpayers were specifically interested in standardized achievement scores, while parents

Table 7.6. Information About Private Choice Schools, Rank-Ordered by Percentage of Taxpayers Who Believe its Reporting Should Be Mandatory

Item	Mandatory (%)	Number Responding		
		Mandatory	Voluntary	Neither
The qualifications of teachers and administrators	85	655	105	11
How money is budgeted and spent	78	300	163	8
The results of an annual financial audit	78	604	149	18
The graduation rate	75	579	173	19
The scores on state standardized tests	75	578	178	15
Student attendance rate	73	566	193	12
The curriculum	73	561	191	19
The school's governing structure	70	542	202	27
The methods of teaching	66	505	248	18
The mission and philosophy of a school	65	501	241	29
Number of students suspended/expelled annually	61	473	275	23
Teacher turnover	55	425	310	36
Class size	55	322	431	18
The requirements for parental involvement	49	381	370	20
The racial or ethnic makeup of the student body	33	257	485	29
The economic background of the student body	29	227	514	30
Graduate placement	27	208	539	24

Note: The items were rotated in order to limit the possibility of bias toward options at the end of the response list. The percentage of Don't Know or Refusal responses for each item varied from 1 percent for How Money Is Budgeted and Spent to 4.7 percent for Teacher Turnover.

and teachers were more interested in general outcomes not limited to test scores. In the school-based interviews, we found that 30 percent of parents were very interested in how well their children do and less interested in aggregate measures of school achievement. Standardized test score results are found to be an important source of information about a school only by 15 percent of parents and 12 percent of teachers. Forty percent of the school administrators we interviewed believed test scores were an important piece of information. For taxpayers, test scores are also important: 75 percent supported mandatory reporting of state standardized test results.

In addition, we found consistency with our stakeholders on the mandatory reporting of graduation rates, which 75 percent of taxpayers support, and on the mandatory reporting of graduate placement, supported by 27 percent of those surveyed.

Some disagreement exists between taxpayers and school-based stakeholders over whether reporting how money is budgeted and spent and whether reporting the results of an annual financial audit should be mandatory. Seventy-eight percent of taxpayers surveyed believed reporting this information should be mandatory. Our school-based stakeholders had a different response. Less than 3 percent of stakeholders indicated that financial information about a school was important. Most of our panel members did not find these results contradictory. As one member commented, "Parents may have less interest in the financial affairs of a school because it is not their money supporting it. Taxpayers, however, want fiscal responsibility when their tax dollars are at issue."

In order to ensure that our findings truly represent consensus, we also determined whether there were any statistically significant differences across other characteristics, including race, gender, income, state of residence, support for private school choice, educational level, and whether the respondent had school-age children.[11] Using a simple difference of means test, we found that regardless of taxpayer differences in race, income level, or support of school choice, there was strong support for mandatory reporting of particular items. The exceptions are discussed below.

We found that compared to whites, African Americans were more likely to support mandatory reporting of the racial or ethnic makeup of the student body (43 percent vs. 32 percent) and the requirements for parent involvement (64 percent vs. 47 percent). We also examined differences by income level. The only area in which we found a statistically significant difference was in support of mandatory reporting of standardized test results. Lower-income respondents were less likely to believe this information should be required. Even given this statistically significant difference, however, we still found two-thirds of low-income respondents supporting mandatory reporting of standardized test scores.

We also looked at differences between individuals who expressed support and those who expressed opposition to school choice programs.[12] Individuals who oppose choice were more likely to support mandatory reporting of the economic background of the student body (40 percent compared to 26 percent), the racial or ethnic makeup of the student body (39 percent compared to 32 percent), and graduate placement (35 percent compared to 25 percent). The portion supporting these mandatory reporting requirements did not exceed 50 percent.

Another hypothesized difference was between parents of school-aged children and other taxpayers. In only one case did we find a statistically significant difference. Parents of school-aged children were more likely than other taxpayers to believe that the methods of teaching should be a mandatory reporting requirement of private schools (73 percent vs. 59 percent). We also looked at differences between parents who send their children to private schools and parents whose children go to public schools. Our sample includes 398 parents with a total of 575 children. Of these children, 17 percent, or 97, attend private schools in Ohio or Wisconsin. This percentage is representative of children in

Ohio and Wisconsin who attend private school. We found no statistically significant differences between these groups. In addition, we looked for differences by state of residence, education level, and gender and did not find any statistically significant differences based on these variables. This degree of consistency in desire for mandatory reporting requirements is important for developing widely acceptable accountability guidelines.

Gathering and Disseminating Information

Our survey of taxpayers also addressed how information about schools should best be disseminated. Specifically, we asked, "If private choice schools are required to report information to the public, somebody has to gather this information and make it available. Do you think (Read organization list below) should be given this job?"

The list of options read to taxpayers included the five items provided to the school-based respondents. These were the state department of education, the private schools themselves, an accreditation agency, a privately run parent information center, or no agency because parents will decide for themselves. Moreover, because of the stakeholders' interest in adding options, two others were included in the list read to taxpayers. These were a public board consisting of representatives from both private choice schools and public schools and a coordinating council made up of representatives of private choice schools.

Like our school-based stakeholders, our taxpayers were generally unsupportive of the proposition of having parents gather school information on their own. As reported in table 7.7, three out of ten taxpayers supported this method. Support for this method was lowest among those individuals that oppose choice, 20 percent, and reached 36 percent for individuals supportive of a universal voucher. Seventy percent of taxpayers surveyed indicated that they believed a board consisting of representatives from both private choice schools and public

Table 7.7. Percentage of Taxpayers Selecting Yes to Question: "Who Should Be Responsible for Gathering Information about Private Schools?" by Support for Vouchers

	Total Respondents	Support Vouchers (Low Income Only)	Support Vouchers (Regardless of Income)	Oppose Vouchers
A public board consisting of representatives from both private choice schools and public schools	70	72	70	69
An accreditation agency that is a membership organization that grants accreditation status to schools	54	54	53	55
The state department of education	53	55	52	57
A coordinating council made up of representatives of private choice schools	47	51	47	43
The private choice schools themselves, rather than an organization	43	48	45	32
A privately run parent information center	37	43	39	27
Individual parents themselves, rather than an organization	33	38	36	20
N	771	180	408	166

Note: The percentage of Don't Know or Refusal responses for each item varied from 4 percent for A Public Board Consisting of Representatives from Both Private Choice Schools and Public Schools to 8 percent for An Accreditation Agency.

schools should be given this task. This method was equally popular regardless of one's support or opposition to choice. Again, this option was not included in our stakeholder interviews. The next most popular options in our taxpayer survey were an accreditation agency and the state department of education. They both received about the same level of support, 54 percent and 53 percent respectively. Again, support remained the same whether a respondent supports or opposes vouchers. These findings are consistent with our school-based stakeholder interviews, in which the accreditation option received support from half of the individuals we interviewed, while two-thirds supported the state department of education. The accreditation model is used at the postsecondary level of education for public and private schools that receive public money for student loans, grants, or scholarships. Accreditation for voucher schools, however, did not receive a consensus of support as an information source. There was also disagreement between taxpayers and school-based stakeholders over a privately run parent information center. Two-thirds of the stakeholders approved of this method but only one-third of the taxpayer respondents did. Moreover, individuals opposed to vouchers were less likely to support this option, at 27 percent, compared to respondents who support vouchers for low-income families, at 43 percent.

Another question we asked of taxpayers but did not include in our school-based stakeholder interviews was, "Of these organizations, please tell me which is the best one to be responsible for this task. I will read you the list." By asking the question in this manner, we required the respondent to make a choice among the available options. Table 7.8 shows the percentage of taxpayers who chose each option and includes a breakdown by respondents' support for vouchers. A board consisting of representatives from both private choice and public schools scored highest as the best agency to collect and disseminate information on private schools. This option received consistent support by both supporters and opponents of vouchers. The state department of education was next, chosen by approximately 25 percent of those surveyed. But support for this option was 7 percentage points higher for opponents of vouchers versus those that support universal vouchers. Other options, including accreditation, were chosen by less than 12 percent of those surveyed. In addition, while overall support for parents gathering this

Table 7.8. Percent of Taxpayers Selecting Item as the "Best" by Support for Vouchers: "Of these organizations, which one is the best one to be responsible for gathering information and making it available?"

	Total Respondents	Support Vouchers (Low Income Only)	Support Vouchers (Regardless of Income)	Oppose Vouchers
Public board consisting of representatives from both private choice and public schools	31	31	29	33
The state department of education	25	26	23	30
Individual parents themselves, rather than an organization	11	14	13	4
An accreditation agency that is a membership organization that grants accreditation status to schools	10	9	11	10
The private choice schools themselves, rather than an organization	8	9	8	6
A coordinating council made up of representatives of private choice schools	7	4	8	7
A privately run parent information center	6	5	6	5
Don't know/refused	2	2	2	5
N	771	180	408	166

information on their own was 11 percent, it was lowest among opponents of vouchers, at 4 percent, and highest among supporters of vouchers for low-income families, at 14 percent.

We further examined these group differences through a simple difference of means test. We found some statistically significant differences in levels of support. For example, as noted, opponents of school choice were less likely to support a privately run parent information center (27 percent compared to 40 percent) as an information source. Opponents were also less likely to support the private choice schools themselves as information disseminators (32 percent compared to 46 percent). Finally, opponents were less likely to support leaving information gathering to the individual parents themselves, rather than an organization (20 percent compared to 37 percent). When we explored whether there were any differences in support for various reporting organizations by income, our results indicated that individuals in the wealthiest category were least likely to support a privately run parent information center (24 percent for high income compared to 38 percent for medium income and 44 percent for low income). Across all income groups, however, less than a majority supported this option. We found little support among high-income respondents for having no organization be responsible and leaving the responsibility up to the parents (21 percent for high income compared to 33 percent for medium income and 41 percent for low income). Again, less than a majority across all income groups supported this option. Finally, there were mixed levels of support across income groups for giving the state department of education this responsibility (50 percent for high income compared to 60 percent for low income).

Schools Must Be Exposed to the Financial Consequences of Parents' Actions

In our face-to-face interviews with school-based stakeholders we did not discuss the consequences of parental actions, primarily because the focus at that time was information needs and dissemination rather than the repercussions of that information gathering. After further discussion by our panel, however, we felt it was necessary to measure support for various scenarios of imposing consequences on schools that failed to provide information because, as explained in chapter 6, schools that are, by policy, insulated from the fiscal effects of competition have little incentive to meet parents' needs. Thus, if the legislatively created market is incapable of penalizing noncomplying schools, schools may need to be exposed to other fiscal penalties to keep the choice system accountable. Therefore, survey questions were added to specifically address what should be done if a school does not follow information-reporting requirements. We asked taxpayers, "In your opinion what should be done if a school does not follow the mandated reporting requirements?" The options included granting a one-year probationary period in order to meet the requirement, imposing a fine, and taking away a school's eligibility for taxpayer money.

While one of the fundamental points that choice supporters often make is that poor schools will fail and that this is the ultimate form of accountability, we found across both supporters and opponents of choice the desire to foster the start-up and participation of voucher schools. Therefore, immediate penalties for noncompliance with reporting requirements were not viewed as helpful to voucher schools or to parents. Eighty-three percent of taxpayer respondents believed schools that do not follow the mandated reporting requirements should be granted a one-year probationary period in order to meet the requirement. Such support was lower for opponents of vouchers, at 79 percent, but still sizable at over three-fourths. Fifty-seven percent of all taxpayers believed a school should lose its eligibility for taxpayer money. This belief was higher for opponents of vouchers, at 68 percent. When we looked at this question by race, we found that African Americans were less likely to believe a school should lose its eligibility for taxpayer funds, at 43 percent, compared to 59 percent for white respondents. Only 36 percent of all taxpayers felt a fine should be given to a noncomplying school. This increased to 40 percent for opponents of vouchers, still well below majority support.

Accountability Guidelines: Divergent Views

At the outset, our purpose was to search for a consensus on the important issue of choice school accountability. Yet given the perceived gap between the opposing sides, we were only moderately optimistic that a consensus could be reached. Thus, it was encouraging and very enlightening that, in a study that included 270 face-to-face interviews and 771 telephone surveys, we were able to develop accountability guidelines that reflect a consensus. In one particular area, however, consensus could not be found and accountability guidelines could not be developed, and that was in school operating requirements. This includes such topics as hiring state-certified teachers, admittance of voucher students, and parental involvement requirements. Table 7.9 lists the questions asked in the taxpayer survey and the percentage that agreed with the statement.

Table 7.9. Percentage of Taxpayers Who Agree "Private Schools Participating in a Choice Program Should . . . ," by Income

	Total	Low <$25,000	Middle $26,000–$60,000	High >$60,000
Be required to hire only state-certified teachers	73	75	72	78
Be required to make their meetings open to the public	86	88	86	84
Be allowed to choose which students they will enroll	35	29*	36*	41*
Be allowed to charge parents for costs above those covered by the taxpayer contribution	66	53*	72*	73*
Be allowed to require parents to volunteer at the school	66	69	65	68
N	771	184	369	121

* Statistically significant difference between groups.

Because we did not find consensus regarding school operations, we outline the various viewpoints we found when talking to stakeholders and taxpayers about this issue.

- *Should schools participating in choice be allowed to require parents to work as volunteers in the school?*

Currently a number of schools participating in choice in both Cleveland and Milwaukee require parents to volunteer time as a part of their admissions requirements (Van Dunk 1998). As one administrator said, "We have a straightforward pledge sheet for 20 hours of parent involvement. Some families have been and [others] will be asked to leave if they are chronic about not contributing." Other administrators view requiring parent involvement as a barrier to participation by some families. Schools have various ways of dealing with parental noncompliance with volunteer requirements, from a fine to no longer letting a child enroll in the school.

Because of the controversy that surrounds this issue, we explored the interest in mandatory reporting of parent involvement requirements both in our interviews with school-based stakeholders and in our taxpayer surveys. In our school-based interviews, there was limited interest in wanting information on parent involvement and/or the requirements for parent involvement—12 percent wanted such information. In our taxpayer survey, we first asked whether it should be mandatory for participating schools to report the requirements for parent involvement. A majority of African Americans, 64 percent, supported reporting this information, compared to 46 percent of white taxpayers. In addition, we asked taxpayers whether they agreed or disagreed with the following statement: "Private schools that participate in a choice program should be allowed to require parents to work as volunteers in the school." Over 65 percent of taxpayers agreed.

- *Should schools that participate in choice be allowed to charge parents for the costs above those covered by the tax-payer contribution?*

Cleveland and Milwaukee deal differently with the issue of charging participating students for tuition costs exceeding the value of the voucher. Currently, in Cleveland the scholarship covers between 75 and 90 percent of tuition; the student's family is responsible for paying the additional tuition. In Milwaukee, voucher schools cannot charge tuition above that covered by the voucher. Some individuals we interviewed believed strongly that private schools participating in choice must be allowed to charge for costs above that covered by the voucher. As one administrator stated at a Wisconsin Assembly Hearing of the Committee on Urban Education on February 28, 1996, "We propose that an enrollment fee of no more than fifty dollars per family would not be too onerous for them and would add value in their eyes to the education their children are receiving. Successful schools have been built on parents sacrificing something." Other administrators argued that participating schools should not charge such fees. Two-thirds of taxpayers surveyed believed participating schools should be able to charge for those costs not covered by the taxpayer contribution. Here, too, we found disagreement between African Americans and whites over the issue of charging additional fees. Less than a majority, 43 percent, of African Americans supported allowing fees or tuition charges compared to 66 percent of whites.

- *When choice schools get more applicants than they have vacancies, should they be allowed to choose which applicants they will enroll or should they be required to conduct a lottery?*

There was some disagreement over whether voucher schools should adhere to strict policies ensuring nondiscrimination based on religion, gender, disability, prior academic achievement, and prior student behavior. Currently, choice schools in Milwaukee are exempted from the Individuals with Disabilities Education Act (IDEA) (Mead 2000). Opponents of school choice argue that selection systems that allow schools to choose whom they enroll will lead to inequality in education. Some proponents, on the other hand, believe that schools should be able to set certain admission standards as long as they do not discriminate on the basis of race or ethnicity.

Our survey results indicate that overall 61 percent of taxpayers believed voucher schools should use a random admission system, whereas approximately 70 percent of taxpayers making less than $25,000 per year thought so. Currently, the choice application guidelines for both Cleveland and Milwaukee contain provisions requiring a lottery system if there are more applicants than spaces.

- *Should schools that participate in choice hire only state-certified (or -licensed) teachers?*

Private schools participating in choice in Cleveland and Milwaukee currently can hire uncertified teachers. But as a private choice school administrator remarked, "It would be difficult for me to recommend to our personnel committee hiring a teacher who is not certified. The person would have to have some special skills that would permit me to recommend the person." There was no consistent support for requiring choice schools to hire only state-licensed teachers. In our school-based stakeholder interviews, parents did not express a high interest in certification as the only means for judging the qualifications of teachers, but taxpayers in our survey overwhelmingly supported this requirement, at 73 percent.

Accountability Guidelines: Consensus Views

Although we found divergent views on the issue of school operating guidelines, the level of agreement among all our interview and survey respondents on information gathering and dissemination issues was such that our panel was able to create three broadly supported guidelines for accountability. The guidelines reflect consensus areas in which we found a strong convergence of support from stakeholders and taxpayers of all backgrounds. We offer these guidelines to policymakers who may tackle the controversial task of creating and enacting accountability mechanisms for school choice programs.

Guideline 1. Schools that participate in choice need to make public the following information: curriculum, graduation rate, how money is budgeted and spent, methods of teaching, mission and philosophy of a school, number of students suspended and expelled annually, qualifications of teachers and administrators, school's governing structure, scores on state standardized tests, and student attendance rate.[13]

The first guideline is aimed at helping parents make informed choices by providing them with needed information. Parents selecting schools want this type of information, and taxpayers who are providing the funds for these schools believe this information should be mandatory.

The informational items included in the guideline have the support of at least 60 percent of taxpayers surveyed. In our face-to-face interviews, information on the school's program and primarily its curriculum and method of instruction are the most common kinds of information valued by parents. Information on teachers is the next most important for parents. The other criteria mentioned are general student outcomes, school characteristics such as class size and makeup of student body, safety and discipline, standardized test scores, level of parental involvement, and the school's reputation. We note that in our survey we found support (at 78 percent) for both "How Money was Budgeted and Spent" and the "Results of Annual Financial Audit." We believe these items cover the same types of information and therefore include only budgeting and spending in this guideline.

In addition, it is worth highlighting some items that are not included in the guideline. One of these is class size. Fifty-five percent of taxpayers in Ohio and Wisconsin said that information on class size should be mandatory. In our school-based interviews class size was categorized as a part of school characteristics and was believed to be an important piece of information by 31 percent of parents, 30 percent of teachers, and 44 percent of administrators. In terms of the information needs of parents, class size is a commonly requested item; however, it did not make the cutoff of 60 percent for a consensus item. Neither did teacher turnover, which was supported by 55 percent of taxpayers in Ohio and Wisconsin. Finally, we do not include mandatory reporting of parent involvement as part of guideline 1 since, even though a majority of African Americans supported it, overall only 49 percent did so. We believe that further discussion of whether this item should be a part of reporting requirements is warranted.

Requiring the reporting of these items ultimately means that schools participating in the voucher program actually gather and collect the information. Nowhere is the opposition to such collection as great as in the area of standardized test scores. Our stakeholder interviews with private school administrators indicated that reporting test scores would be an added financial cost to the school. Since the time of our interviews some schools participating in the Milwaukee voucher program have implemented a policy of taking the WKCE. Among these are a number of schools that are members of the archdiocese of Milwaukee.[14] Considering the fact that 33 current voucher schools are members of the archdiocese, we anticipate that by the end of 2002 more than one-third of participating voucher schools will be taking the state standardized exams. Hoxby notes in her study of the cost of accountability that comprehensive tests are quite affordable (Hoxby 2002).

Guideline 2. A public-private board consisting of representatives of private choice schools and public schools should be created to gather the required information about choice schools and make it available to the public.

Our second guideline focuses on how best to disseminate information to parents. We feel there is consensus to create a public-private entity to gather and disseminate accurate information from voucher schools. In the school-based interviews we find that stakeholders support a privately run parent information center (64 percent), and to a lesser extent the state department of education (54 percent) or an accreditation agency (50 percent) for this responsibility. Stakeholders were not specifically asked about a public-private board. It was because of the comments made by a number of our stakeholders, however, that this item was included in our taxpayer survey. As we show in table 7.7 above, in our taxpayer survey we found overwhelming support for a board with mixed representation from the private and public schools (70 percent). The next most popular reporting option, the accreditation agency, received support from 54 percent of taxpayers followed by the state department of education at 53 percent.

Creation of a public-private board is not a new idea. Chubb and Moe discuss the need to disseminate information through parent information centers (1990: 221). Moreover, around the country researchers discussing school choice have highlighted the need for broad dissemination of information about schools by a neutral body (Carver and Salganik 1991; Maynard et al. 2002). A public-private board ensures independence from state departments of education, which in some states, for example, Wisconsin, are perceived as being hostile to school choice.[15] Moreover, the public-private combination allows distance from privately run parent information centers,which others may believe are biased by whatever funding agency directly oversees the group.

Guideline 3. Private choice schools that do not follow the reporting require-
ments should be granted a one-year probationary period in order to meet
the requirement. Failure to comply after one year could result in loss of
taxpayer funds.

In our surveys, we found a culture of patience when dealing
with voucher schools. Unlike the market ideal that poor schools should
close, taxpayers felt the need to grant schools time to meet accountability
requirements. In our stakeholder interviews we did not ask about specific mechanisms for enforcing compliance with the reporting requirements. Yet, the comments by those interviewed indicated that schools,
especially new schools, should be given time to establish themselves.

As policymakers tackle this issue, how they implement the enforcement process is a critical component. One possibility is that enforcement could be a function of a state department of education or
public instruction. But if this organization is viewed as taking one side
or the other on the issue of vouchers, then another nonpartisan entity
should be entrusted with that task. Regardless of the chosen entity, enforcement could result from an annual review of the information or
lack of it made available to the public-private information board.

Conclusion

Is it possible to build a consensus on choice school accountability that combines the needs of parents and taxpayers in a way that im-
proves the possibility that competition will lead to real educational improvement? These findings emphatically show that the answer is yes.
Our search for consensus led first to those individuals directly affected
by school choice in Cleveland and Milwaukee and let them tell us what
kinds of information they needed to know about a school. This information was used to create a survey administered to 771 taxpayers in Ohio
and Wisconsin.

The data obtained through our interviews and surveys revealed a consensus for the creation of three specific accountability guidelines for voucher schools. These guidelines should satisfy both the informational needs of parents and the collective needs of taxpayers to hold voucher schools accountable. As policymakers grapple with the important issue of school choice accountability, we hope the guidelines presented in this chapter can help clarify that debate.

We also explored other issues related to possible requirements for choice schools. On the issues of parental involvement requirements, open board meetings, charging of additional fees, admission policies, and teacher certification no consensus was discernable. These issues deserve further study. Answers should satisfy two requirements: first, the need expressed by many individuals that the guidelines not overly restrict the individuality of choice schools, and, second, the need expressed by many others to ensure that taxpayer money is used wisely.

CHAPTER EIGHT

Unleashing the Power of School Choice Through Accountability

A s we were writing the conclusion to this book, a parent called seeking information about voucher schools. Because of our work at the Public Policy Forum in collecting information about voucher schools, we receive calls from parents every week. Parents are referred to the Forum by such institutions as MPS, by local elected officials, by people familiar with our research, and as a result of the directory of voucher schools we distribute annually to local libraries. The Forum never intended to be a day-to-day source of information about voucher schools. Yet it became rapidly evident that the basic information we collect for our annual voucher school directory was in demand by parents and others who called. As a result, the call we received from this parent was far from unique.

Jane (not her real name) is the mother of a daughter who was entering eighth grade. The daughter had, in the words of her mother, "refused to go back to the MPS middle school she attended last spring and was enrolled for this school year." We could overhear the daughter in the background while her mother spoke, making comments about not going back to "that school," and wanting to "enroll in a private school." It was unclear whether the daughter had recently made this declaration or if it was something they had struggled with for some time. The timing was nonetheless poor. Public school was starting in four days, and many private voucher schools would be starting their semester the following week. That Jane was exasperated by her daughter's refusal was clear, and her urgent desire to find a private school was easily detectable.

Jane had called several schools that were listed in our directory to find out if they were enrolling eighth grade students. Two of the schools Jane called were taking only eighth grade voucher students who had previously attended the school's seventh grade, but she had found two others that were still enrolling eighth graders. Jane said she had visited both of them. She called the Forum for the same reason that many parents call the Forum—she wanted to know more about the schools. Specifically, she wanted to know if the schools hired certified teachers and what their performance was compared to other public and private schools.

The answer we gave was our standard response: The voucher program consists of independent private schools that are not required to provide this information to the public. We mentioned that she should contact the schools again to see if they would share with her performance information and the qualifications of their teachers. We felt that our inability to provide information increased her anxiety. Jane explained that she did not feel her visits gave her a full sense of what the schools were about. As she put it, "I wasn't that impressed with the staff I saw, but it is summer and I just don't know if I can judge them." She went on to say that she wanted more information so she could be more discerning. It was evident that her daughter was pressuring her to let her attend one of these private schools and yet she was quite uneasy about the situation. She noted that she was contemplating giving one of these voucher schools six weeks. Then, if the school did not work out, she would withdraw her daughter and return her to public school. She also made it clear that moving her daughter from one school to another midsemester was not something she really wanted to do.

This parent, like so many others, wanted to improve the educational opportunities for her daughter. The voucher program gave her hope of doing that. Yet she was clearly questioning the adequacy of the education in the two private voucher schools that she visited.

This mother's frustration over her lack of information is not unusual. Since we began receiving calls two years ago, the Forum has received and logged more than two hundred parent calls. In addition, we have distributed seven thousand poster-sized directories to local libraries listing basic information on voucher schools. The number of calls and directories is a testament to the popularity of a program that offers educational choices for hundreds of children whose parents are dissatisfied with their present schooling option. Yet, do such educational choices equate with educational improvement? For Jane, the choices she contemplated did not necessarily answer that question because she did not have adequate information to make the kind of decision she desired. Her situation reflects a major flaw in the structure of the Milwaukee voucher school program, in which competition based on parental choices is expected to hold schools accountable but in which the basic tenets of competition too often are weak or nonexistent.

Some may suggest that such a stark conclusion is premature. *The evidence we have presented in this book, however, makes a forceful case that school choice will not consistently improve education unless some structured accountability is included in choice policies.* Vouchers will not lead to the improvements desired by their proponents unless voucher schools and public schools are able to clearly understand the implications of gaining or losing students; parents are able to have reliable, accurate information to support their schooling choices; and schools are financially rewarded or penalized for gaining or losing students.

Relying on a broad array of data sources, we have documented that in Milwaukee currently parents are unable, by themselves, to hold schools fully accountable. We have sorted through enrollment information for each of the 124 voucher schools that have participated in the voucher program. We have followed over time the movement of these students and documented clearly the weak relationship between accountability and supply and demand. Hundreds of public school teachers in Milwaukee were surveyed to assess the impacts of competition, perceived or real, on their educational practices and whether competition is positively related to any changes made. No such positive relationship was found. Even more troubling is the fact that overall public student performance as measured by achievement on state standardized tests has not improved with increased competition.

Parents were surveyed and parent-researchers sent into schools to enable us to better understand the knowledge parents had about schools and what they could learn by actually visiting schools. These exercises demonstrated the following: (1) overall, parental knowledge of specific schools tends to be low; (2) parents face considerable barriers in their efforts to obtain information about specific schools; and (3) if parental knowledge is the foundation of a competitive educational marketplace, then there is a great deal still to be desired.

We dissected the complex public funding formula for education in Wisconsin in an attempt to understand the relationship between gaining or losing students because of choice, and the financial impact such change has on school funding. In the end, it appears the financial formula supporting choice in Wisconsin was designed to insulate schools from the possible competitive effects that proponents of choice believe should financially reward success while penalizing failure. We highlight these findings below.

Supply and Demand Are Poor Accountability Mechanisms

The relationship between parents' demands and desires and the success or failure of voucher schools is tenuous. In an education marketplace, parents' freedom to choose should identify which schools are good and put bad schools out of business. We document in the beginning of this book, however, that if limits are put on parents' ability to choose schools, accountability based on parents' actions does not work. In the worst case, gains or losses of voucher students mean virtually nothing, making it difficult to hold choice schools accountable through parental actions alone.

One such limit on parents' choices presents itself when there is only a weak link between accountability and supply and demand. The data we highlight demonstrate that the supply of voucher seats is constrained, leading to an artificial notion of demand. In other words, by controlling supply, schools can also control demand. For example, we know that many large, popular private schools have relatively few voucher students, suggesting that some schools, choosing to maintain their tuition-based enrollment, may cap the number of voucher seats. We also know that schools leaving the choice program do not do so because voucher parents are not choosing them; more than four hundred voucher students have chosen schools that failed to participate in the program the following year. In only one case over the past eleven years was the closure of a choice school the direct result of parental action, but the parents who acted were not voucher parents; they were tuition-paying parents who left the school to form a new one. Finally, we know that each year at least one quarter of voucher students do not use a voucher the following year and are replaced in even greater numbers by new voucher students, resulting in student movement that does not hold individual schools accountable.

Milwaukee's choice program is based on the premise that parents' actions will lead to an accountability system in which good schools succeed and poor schools fail. The data available offer no evidence that this is happening thus far in Milwaukee. Choice schools do not supply voucher seats in response to parents' demands. Parents' choices do not drive schools to improve or close.

Public Schools Have Not Responded to Competition

The vast majority of students in our country attend public schools, mostly on an assigned basis. The theory behind publicly funded private school choice is that competition will motivate public schools to improve. To discover if this is happening, we examined whether any changes in educational practices and performance are occurring in MPS that could be attributed to the presence of voucher schools. No demonstrable relationship was found.

Over the past two school years, despite a 400 percent increase in enrollment in Milwaukee's private school voucher program, no predictable patterns emerge relative to changes in public school educational practices. Any increases in staff awareness of competition, changes in school climate, and efforts made by schools to retain or attract students are unrelated to actual competition from voucher schools. Finally, increased voucher competition does not appear to be related to increases in student reading or math achievement over the past three years.

The result is that in Milwaukee, parents are not receiving the promised educational benefits of competition through school choice.

Empowered Parents Need Information

School choice has the potential to give parents, rather than the government, ultimate responsibility for school accountability. To be thus empowered, parents must possess accurate information about the schools they choose. We hypothesized that in choice systems in which there are few outside accountability mechanisms, parents should have a greater incentive to seek accurate information and should be more consistent in the messages their choices send to schools and to other parents. We surveyed parents who had chosen a school and found that, regardless of the type of choice program they participate in, parents are largely uninformed about many characteristics of the schools their children attend. Moreover, we found choice systems differ only slightly in the extent to which they motivate parents to seek information. Well-informed parents are scarce, and they are no more likely to be found in traditional, tuition-based private school choice systems than in public school choice systems. A school choice system that functions on the pure competitive market theory that well-informed, knowledgeable parents and their resulting choices are all that is necessary to hold schools accountable falls short in Milwaukee. Private school parents, who could be expected to have a deeper interest in their schools than public school parents, for whom outside accountability mechanisms already exist, are no better informed than their public school counterparts. Again, reality does not uphold the promise of the competitive market theory of accountability.

Procuring Information When Shopping for Schools Is Difficult

Why are parents relatively ill-informed about the schools their children attend? There are two answers to that question. One is that parents may not make the effort to obtain information. The other is that information is difficult to obtain. As one test of the latter, we attempted to duplicate what highly motivated parents, those who actively seek out information by visiting schools, experience. We sent parent-researchers shopping for schools.

They visited a representative sample of 41 voucher schools enrolling more than 3,500 voucher students. The reports from these parent-researchers indicated much inconsistency among voucher schools in their ability or willingness to provide information and serve their prospective "customers." A number of schools made it exceedingly difficult to obtain information from them. Why schools that supposedly are in a competitive environment would resist assisting inquiring parents is unclear. Whether these barriers are intentional or not does not matter. The result is the same—some parents will be forced to make a schooling decision with limited information.

The fact that these barriers exist does little to bolster the case that parents on their own are capable of holding voucher schools accountable. Without solid, accurate, easily obtainable information, parents are vulnerable—not empowered.

Reaping the Wrong Rewards: The Dollars Do Not Follow the Child

One of the main reasons private school choice programs are so controversial is the belief held by many voucher opponents that such programs drain badly needed money away from public schools. After all, competition for students and the accompanying dollars is at the core of a market-based system. In a market-based system, public schools should improve if they are forced to compete with private schools for taxpayer dollars. If the dollars follow the child, then clear winners and losers will emerge.

We tested whether this system works in Milwaukee through an extensive analysis of Wisconsin's educational funding mechanism. Our findings show that Wisconsin's funding formula for vouchers was designed to insulate the public schools from possible negative effects of competition. The reason is that the education funding pie in Wisconsin grew to accommodate voucher students whose private school education previously did not cost the state. Quirks in the funding mechanism lead districts that are hundreds of miles away from voucher competition to feel they are losing money to voucher schools. But the financial impact on the only public school district that directly competes with voucher schools—MPS—has been negligible.

In addition, voucher income has had a positive financial impact on all participating private schools. Yet if the program were operating as a true market, we should see a negative effect as well. Vouchers have instead been a subsidy, as parents who had previously been paying private tuition took advantage of vouchers. Schools that could not survive on private tuition turned to vouchers. And a continuous flow of new students into the voucher program so far has reduced the competitive impact of the relatively high rate of students leaving the system—approximately 25 percent annually in the aggregate.

While the funding of vouchers has been embraced politically, the politics of public education in Wisconsin ensured that MPS and the state's public schools in general would be insulated from real financial harm. No legislator wanted to be the bearer of bad tidings in his or her home district. The result is that state policymakers never created a zero-sum system in which dollars truly followed the child. What operates in Milwaukee is nothing like the free-market system envisioned by vouchers' strongest advocates. Therefore, there should be no expectation that schools will have much financial incentive to compete by improving their performance.

Improving Education through Better Accountability

If publicly funded private school vouchers were meant only to provide low-income parents with more choices for their children, then the case we have stated regarding competition and accountability would be of little concern. Parental satisfaction would be measure enough. But the promotion of school choice vouchers has been about so much more. Proponents of vouchers have cast choice as a way of improving overall educational performance through market competition and by shifting decision making from monopolistic central administrative offices to parent-consumers. Parents, armed with information and financial vouchers, become the arbiters of power and accountability, determining by their decisions the success or failure of schools. That is the great and justifiable promise of school choice.

The reality of the Milwaukee experience has been far different.

For parents to hold schools accountable, they need to be well informed. But as we have demonstrated, most are not. Available information is not uniform and in many cases is either not easily obtainable or nonexistent. Schools do not necessarily respond to parental demands. State educational financing holds schools immune to competitive pressures from voucher schools. The result is that parents are not truly empowered. Their decisions alone do not hold schools accountable. In the absence of supporting mechanisms of accountability, competition does not work and the hoped-for educational improvements do not materialize.

Recommendations for Accountability

We suggest steps that can be taken to strengthen accountability and repair the voucher program so that it can live up to its promise. These steps represent recommendations drawn from stakeholders involved with choice and from the tax-paying public at large. We believe these guidelines satisfy both the informational needs of parents and the collective needs of taxpayers to hold voucher schools accountable. We believe that they can be shaped in a manner that will not threaten the individuality and self-determination that differentiates private from public schools.

Having accurate knowledge about educational options, parents can reduce their anxiety in selecting a school and make decisions that truly fit the needs of their children. Therefore, our first guideline for improving access to information is to *make public for all participating schools, the following minimum information: the school's curriculum, the graduation rate, how money is budgeted and spent, the methods of teaching, the school's mission and philosophy, the number of students suspended and expelled annually, the qualifications of teachers and administrators, the school's governing structure, scores on state standardized tests, and the student attendance rate.*

Information should not only be available, but easily accessible to parents and the public. It should be accurate and credible. Our second guideline is thus *the creation of a public/private entity consisting of representatives of private schools and public schools to gather and disseminate information from voucher schools.* By requiring schools to report information and having that information disseminated through a public/private agency, the cost to parents of information acquisition is significantly lowered, and parents are thereby truly empowered. The specific mechanism for disseminating this information should be explored by policymakers; there are several options. In Wisconsin, for example, for all public schools data on staffing, student performance, expenditures and revenues are made available in publicly accessible Internet-based databases. See, for example, *http://www.dpi.state.wi.us/dpi/stats.html* for a sample of the statistics maintained by the Wisconsin DPI. Perhaps voucher school data could be added to these databases. As another example, the public/private agency may operate a walk-in resource and information center.

Unfortunately, some schools may not be interested in or may not be able to share such information. In the interests of parents and taxpayers alike, we recommend a final guideline: *Private choice schools that do not provide accurate information should be granted a one-year probationary period to meet the requirement. Failure to comply after one year should result in loss of taxpayer funds.* Immediate penalties for noncompliance with reporting requirements were not viewed as helpful to voucher schools or to parents. There was overwhelming support for granting a probationary period of one year to schools in order to allow them to meet the requirements. Enforcement most likely would be a function of the state department of education, though other entities could also be considered. An annual review of the information gathered by the public/private information agency would reveal whether any voucher schools are not in compliance.

The three guidelines we suggest do not overly restrict the operation of the private, independent schools participating in the school choice program, yet they ensure that taxpayer money is used wisely and that parents are truly empowered.

Unleashing the Power of School Choice

Few books written about vouchers can resist the temptation to focus anecdotally on children who rise from the depths of poverty to the top sphere of success through the use of a voucher. Others may document the plight of children who use a voucher believing that it is a ticket out of a terrible educational system only to find that vouchers are just another empty promise. These overused stories of forlorn children can be both demeaning and unfair because they sensationalize the extremes without examining the countless families whose lives cannot be summed up with clever analogies. We resist that temptation.

Instead, we document from several different angles the limitations of accountability when it is based solely on parental actions. Such actions alone cannot lead to the hoped-for competitive environment in which success and failure are easily identifiable and sustainable. In fact, absent outside accountability, we should never anticipate that such a competitive environment could arise.

Our conclusion that vouchers can never live up to their promise without outside accountability might be dismissed by pure market theorists as another attempt to end school choice. That is certainly one possibility, although we believe it is an unlikely one. Dismissing the need for outside accountability ignores what the voucher movement was all about in the first place. The promise of vouchers is about improving education. It is a promise that we believe has the potential to be achieved if accountability is addressed sufficiently. Therefore, we feel our documentation of the Milwaukee experience can allow vouchers to reform education.

Vouchers are about using competition to improve education—competition that is unleashed by giving parents the ability to select schools for their children rather than having that decision made by someone else. Such competition is negated or distorted when parents are left in the vulnerable position of making choices with limited or inaccurate information and with no assurance that their decisions will result in real educational improvement for their children.

Public schools offer a wide array of educational quality. In any city there are both high-performing public schools and low-performing public schools. If parents are given no choice, then some parents will be lucky enough to have their children attend the high-performing schools and others will be forced to have their children attend low-performing schools. Vouchers are supposed to turn this system upside down. Yet, without adequate accountability, instead of reforming this system vouchers will merely replicate it. If school choice is about empowering parents so they can improve education, then accountability gives real strength to that choice. Without it, parental choices alone cannot ensure that we do not substitute faltering public schools where no choice is available with faltering private schools that are chosen.

Notes

CHAPTER 2. *Parental Choice, Parental Power, and Accountability*

1. The contracts require a number of things such as occupancy permits, licensure, and background checks of teachers as well as participation in state mandated standardized testing. In 2000–01 there are seventeen schools with contracts for at-risk students, one special education school, six adjudicated youth schools, and four behavior reassignment contracts. Contact is Wayne Berzinski at MPS Small Community Schools.

2. When the MPCP legislation was expanded if a student was already enrolled in a private school, in order to qualify for a voucher the student would have to have been in kindergarten through third grade in 1995. Thus by the year 2009 eligibility requires that in the previous school year the pupil was enrolled in a public school in Milwaukee or was not enrolled in school.

3. This excludes the sixty-four seniors who would automatically leave the program in the spring of 1999.

4. This excludes the sixty seniors who would automatically leave the program in the spring of 2000.

CHAPTER 3. *The Response of Public Schools to Competition*

1. For no question was race a significant factor.

2. To ensure that answers referred only to changes at a teacher's current school, we asked how long a teacher had been at his or her current school. There was no significant difference in the results, however, when teachers who had been at their current school less than two years were excluded from the sample. Therefore, all reported results include these teachers.

3. We should note that while MPCP is the largest and most talked about choice program in Milwaukee, two other new choice programs were imple-

mented in 1988–99: public school Open Enrollment and the Milwaukee Charter School Program. During the time of our survey only 787 total students were participating in these two other choice programs. In addition, two other long-running choice programs affect thousands of Milwaukee students each year. The MPS' within-district open enrollment program has allowed parents to partici-pate in a three-choice selection process for their children since 1990. Addition-ally, since 1976 minority parents in Milwaukee have had the option of sending their children to one of 23 suburban districts via the state's interdistrict Chapter 220 integration program. Neither of these programs grew during the time under study. In addition, charter schools were just starting in Milwaukee at this time, and only three were operating. The existence of several choice programs in Mil-waukee results in an environment of competition unmatched in the nation. But it is the expansion of the voucher program that has garnered the most attention and, for the timeframe of our survey, had the most participants. Therefore, to understand the impact of competition on the public school system we focus primarily on voucher schools.

4. As noted in table 3.2, these questions include changes in the past two years or so in use of outside classroom resources, teaching methods used, daily time management, yearly scheduling, and classroom curriculum. The variable ranges from 1 to 5 with a mean score of 2.99 and standard deviation of .77. Cronbach's alpha for the autonomy index is .85. Cronbach's alpha is a numerical coefficient of reliability. Computation of alpha is based on the reliability of a question relative to other questions with the same number of items and measur-ing the same construct of interest (Hatcher 1994). Alpha coefficient ranges from 0 to 1. The higher the score, the more reliable the generated scale is, with .7 being an acceptable reliability coefficient though lower thresholds are sometimes used (Nunnaly 1978).

5. Change in empowerment ranges from 1 to 5 with a mean score of 2.66 and standard deviation of .82.

6. Consumer response ranges from 0 to 2 with a mean score of 1.39 and standard deviation of .52.

7. Collaboration ranges from 1 to 4 with a mean score of 2.94 and standard deviation of .53.

8. The school climate questions ask whether, in the past two school years, the school has established new partnerships with outside organizations, offered new curricular course(s), offered before or after school care, or developed a new school mission. The variable ranges from 0 to 2 with a mean score of 1.37 and standard deviation of .36. Cronbach's raw alpha for school climate is .68, just below the recommended cutoff of .7. A more important issue with school cli-mate, however, is the number of teachers that respond "Don't Know" to these issues. Because over a quarter of the teachers respond "Don't Know" to several

school climate questions we lose 135 cases or 30 percent of our sample when we average the responses to the questions to construct school climate as a dependent variable. We report the OLS coefficients for this model with the caveat that measuring change in school climate may best be assessed by surveying principals or administrators who may have a clearer understanding of what changes have taken place in the school.

9. It is coded 1 if a teacher reports the staff at his or her school discusses the possible impacts of competition on enrollment, 0 otherwise.

10. It is a dummy variable that equals 1 if the teacher indicates the school has, in the past two school years or so, made changes to retain or attract students, 0 otherwise.

11. We also ran the analysis using z scores to measure autonomy, empowerment, consumer response, school climate, and collaboration variables with no change in results. In addition, we ran an exploratory factor analysis on the variables included within each construct. Factor analysis is sometimes used to construct measures of abstract, complicated phenomena where researchers may be uncertain about the domain to be measured. It is especially helpful when the researchers are uncertain about how the measures are related (Buttolph-Johnson and Joslyn 1995). There were no changes in the significance of the models or independent relationships using factor analysis. For our purposes, factor analysis obfuscates the final output since most readers lack familiarity with this statistical technique. For these reasons, the dependent variable in the final model is an average of the variables measuring each construct. Given the fact that our analysis produced consistent results over repeated measurements of the dependent variable, we are confident in the reliability of our measurement of the dependent variables.

12. We also tried other measures of competitive presence, including the number of full-time voucher students enrolled within a half mile of the respondent's school and a continuous variable of 0 to 5 to measure the number of nearby voucher schools. Neither alternative measure of competitive threat provided statistically significant results.

13. As noted above we surveyed teachers with at least seven years of experience in education. The results of our pretesting of the survey instrument led us to make this decision so as to minimize the effects of change that could occur from a less experienced teacher gaining professional confidence. Data for this variable were taken from the DPI.

14. Teacher stability data were not available for 1997–98.

15. Grade level is coded into four separate categories, elementary, kindergarten through eighth grade, middle school, and high school.

16. Initially, we also controlled for a school's student mobility, defined as the average student mobility from 1997–98 to 1999–2000, and a school's percent

poverty, defined as the average percent of the student body that was eligible for free or reduced-price lunch from 1997–98 to 1999–2000. Neither of these variables resulted in statistically significant results.

17. We counted only those voucher schools within a half-mile radius that offered similar grade levels as that particular MPS school. We also ran the analysis using the number of full-time students enrolled in voucher schools within a half-mile radius and found no differences from the results reported above.

18. Since OLS can be an inappropriate technique when the dependent variable is a dummy variable, we also ran our models for discussion of competition and making changes to retain or attract students using logistic regression. The statistical results are the same, and the statistical significance of the independent variables remains the same. To ease interpretation across the models, we report only the coefficients for OLS regression analysis.

19. We did not analyze the scores of the public high schools because the low number of private high schools participating in MPCP would bias our results against the impacts of competition.

20. Our results differ from those of Rouse (1998) and Witte (1999), primarily because those analyses compare the performance of MPS students with the performance of voucher students and because only three voucher schools were included in the research.

21. We also ran a full model in an attempt to see if competition had any effect on change in performance after controlling for several other independent control variables. These independent variables were change in percentage of African American students, change in percentage of students eligible for free or reduced-price lunch, student mobility, administrative tenure, and change in enrollment. As expected (on the basis of the bivariate analysis), competition remained insignificant, and thus we do not report the full models.

22. Our results differ from recent research on Milwaukee. Hoxby's results are couched in terms of school productivity, which she defines as achievement per dollar spent in a school, and presented as school-level results. While she uses school-level test score data, she has no school-level spending data and so uses district-level data (Hoxby 2003). In addition, Hoxby does not use a direct measure of competition, instead defining potential competition as the percent of a public school's enrollment that is low income and ignoring the actual level of competition for any particular school, or even for the city itself on the whole (Hoxby 2003). This is problematic because there have never been enough voucher school seats to accommodate all of Milwaukee's low-income students, even if every such student desired a voucher. Similarly, Gardner's results are not comparable, as he analyzes only a few years' worth of districtwide achievement data and does not include years in which MPS test scores declined (Gardner 2002).

CHAPTER 4. *An Examination of Informed Consumers*

1. An earlier version of this chapter appeared in *Urban Affairs Review* (July 2002).

2. John F. Witte was appointed in 1990 as the State of Wisconsin evaluator of the Milwaukee voucher program. He collected the data used by Manna and others (see *http://dpls.dacc.wisc.edu/choice/*).

3. Charter schools and open enrollment are relatively new in Milwaukee. The Wisconsin Charter School Law was created in 1993. From 1993–97 only one charter school existed in the city. In 1997 the state legislature authorized the City of Milwaukee, the University of Wisconsin-Milwaukee, and the Milwaukee Area Technical College to grant charters. During the time of our survey, 186 students were attending one of four charter schools in Milwaukee. Open enrollment started in Wisconsin in the 1998–99 school year. During the time of our survey, 119 Milwaukee students were participating in this program.

4. The statute defines "minority group pupil" as "a pupil who is Black American, a Native American, a Spanish-surnamed American or an Oriental American." See Julie Mead's report: "Publicly Funded School Choice Options in Milwaukee: An Examination of the Legal Issues," June 2000, Public Policy Forum, Milwaukee, for more information on this program.

5. The list of private school parents came from a list MPS maintains for transportation services. The list includes parents whose schools have worked out transportation agreements with MPS, and parents who have individually requested information from MPS. It is only a small sample, less than 10 percent, of those students who attend private schools in Milwaukee. This list included seventeen parents who identify themselves as having children who receive vouchers.

6. We surveyed the parent or guardian who was responsible for making the educational decisions in the household.

7. We were unable to receive from MPS phone numbers of any of the parents. For this reason, we used a different strategy to get a sample of phone numbers. We asked for and obtained mailing labels for 5,100 students attending or applied to attend suburban schools under the Chapter 220 program, 540 suburban students attending MPS under 220, 4,970 students attending MPS, and 2,122 students attending private school. Since we were conducting a phone survey, the mailing addresses were processed through a reverse directory to obtain telephone numbers. This process involved matching addresses with phone numbers located on a web-based data set. We were able to get phone numbers for 44 percent of the mailing labels. For a number of reasons, phone numbers will not be available for some addresses. First, unlisted numbers were not available. Second, in other cases there was no working phone connected with an address. Finally, the labels represent students, not households; due to the pres-

ence of siblings approximately 38 percent of the addresses are duplicates. We contracted Lein/Spiegelhoff, Inc., a survey research company in Brookfield, Wisconsin, to interview the parent or guardian who makes the decisions about the education of the children living in the household. If the person was not available a callback was set up. Three callbacks were conducted. The completion rate for phone interviews was about 20 percent over the total sample. This means that for every five numbers, one interview was completed. In order to complete 678 interviews, approximately 4,700 phone numbers were needed. Approximately 22 percent, or 1,330 of the numbers, were not accurate for the choice groups. Of the 3,270 accurate phone numbers approximately 7 percent of the attempts resulted in refusal; other interviews were not completed because the interviewer reached an answering machine or voice mail, a busy signal, fax machine, a business number, or a privacy manager.

8. Given the small number of parents we interviewed who participated in the Suburban 220 program we interpret these results with caution. The final numbers in this choice group are useful only for descriptive purposes.

9. We also asked parents if they had knowledge about class size. But we could not examine accuracy of information for this variable because data on class size does not exist for any of these schools. The ratio of teachers to students does exist, but this measure is not a good substitute for class size (see Educational Series on Class Sizes, www.weac.org/sage/research/CLASSIZE.HTM).

10. Reading data for suburban school districts were obtained from the 1999 School Facts Book, published by the Wisconsin Taxpayers' Alliance. These scores include the percentage of students proficient or above on Wisconsin's Knowledge and Concepts Exam, given to fourth, eighth, and tenth graders. The scores are districtwide for Chapter 220 school districts. For MPS schools the data were taken from the 1998–99 MPS Accountability Report published by MPS Division of Research and Assessment. Private schools are not required to take these standardized exams and therefore are not included in this analysis. Data for public schools on percentage of school that is African American are taken from the same sources listed above. For private schools these data were taken from the schools themselves, many of whom report racial makeup on the Empowering Parents for Informed Choices in Education website. This information was also obtained from the 2000 Legislative Audit Report for schools in which MPCP students made up at least 90 percent of the student body. Finally, data on students receiving free or reduced-price lunch were taken from the Wisconsin DPI. This information is for both private and public schools.

11. Controlling for the individual level characteristics of parents, we examined logistic regression models for accuracy of information. None of the models approached statistical significance. Because these models are not significant, the fact that these questions were asked of half of the survey respondents, and the

lack of reading score data for private schools we do not include the models in this chapter.

12. We acknowledge that the error would be higher if we tested whether the respondent was correct.

13. We also examined these differences by grade level and found no significant differences.

14. Our sample was made up of 43 percent white, 39 percent African American, 8 percent Hispanic, 5 percent Asian, and 3 percent other. In addition, 3 percent of our survey respondents refused to answer. We ran the model using all five categories; there were no statistically significant differences between the nonwhite categories.

15. Our survey question on education provided us with five categories. Six percent of our total sample had less than a high school degree, 24 percent a high school degree, 36 percent some college/tech school, 33 percent graduated from college and/or had some postgraduate work. We ran this analysis with separate dummy variables for each grouping and did not find statistically significant differences for categories less than a college degree. For this reason the final model is a dummy variable.

16. The distribution of respondents across our income variable is as follows: 0–$10,999 = 5 percent, $11,000–$19,999 = 9 percent, $20,000–$29,999 = 15 percent, $30,000–$39,999 = 13 percent, $40,000–$49,999 = 13 percent, $50,000–$59,999 = 11 percent, $60,000–$69,999 = 10 percent, and > $70,000 = 10 percent.

17. We asked, "How often do you go to a place of worship?" Our distribution of responses included 18 percent who go more than once a week, 35 percent who go at least once a week, 21 percent who go at least once a month, 13 percent who go at least once a year, and 10 percent who never go or go less than once a year.

18. Length of residence was included as an independent variable because parents who have resided in a district may know more about the schools their children will attend than parents who are new to the district.

19. Besides exploring the impact of the independent variables, it is instructive to examine several goodness of fit measures that the logistic regression procedure generates. In logistic regression, the analog of the global F test is a likelihood ratio chi-square test statistic, which is often referred to as the model chi square. We test H_0, all the betas equal 0, against H_1, at least one beta is not 0. This test statistic is 74 with 19 df significant (p. < .0001) for both models. Thus we can conclude that at least one of the betas in the model is nonzero. The logistic regression technique also produces predictions of the actual dependent variable. The results indicate that the model explaining knowledge of the principal is correct 74 percent of the time. The model also includes a measure of how well the model reduces prediction error using the variables included in the

model versus when predicted by chance alone. We report the Somers' D statistic. We reduce error by 48 percent (see Damaris 1992 and Hosmer and Lemeshow 1989 for a further discussion of logit modeling).

20. Selectivity bias is a concern whenever the assignments to the treatment and control groups are not random (Barnow 1980: 43–45). One method to examine the possible impact of selectivity bias is to run a two-staged least squares (2SLS) regression model. This method has been used when the factors related to selection into a group are known. It is also useful when examining one treatment group and one control group (Barnow et al. 1980; Heckman 1980; and see Schneider, Teske, and Marshall 2000 and Witte 2000 for use of 2SLS in choice studies). This method is not necessary for the models examined in this book. First, parents are selecting themselves into separate programs, not one. Second, all the individuals studied are active choosers. As Schneider, Teske, and Marshall found, when all the parents in the program must choose, nonrandom self-selection does not apply (2000: 83). Third, the final model is not an OLS, but a logistic regression model. The two-stage regression procedure when modeled for this analysis produced estimates that were substantively meaningless. For these reasons we report the final logistic model. This does not mean that selectivity bias has not been adequately addressed. What it does mean is that the best way to minimize the impact in this study was to ensure that factors related to being an informed consumer were included as control variables. As Barnow (1980) notes, the most common way to deal with selectivity bias is to make a diligent effort to include a large number of independent variables that control for selection bias. Every attempt was made to include survey questions that would ensure no variables related to the dependent variable were excluded. In this way we feel confident an omitted variable would not account for the differences among these programs.

21. Because of the difficulty in interpreting logit coefficients, we report the log odds ratio.

22. The chi-square test statistic is 34.8 with 19df and is significant ($p <$ .01). The model is correct 66 percent of the time in predicting a mixed signal. The Somers' D statistic suggests that we reduce prediction error by 33 percent.

23. We ran both logistic regression models, knowledge of parents and mixed signals, using parents who select regular MPS schools as the reference group. The models are estimated by using the same independent variables, and the several goodness of fit measures are identical. The only statistically significant relationship is between parents participating in the MPS Chapter 220 program and the reference group (parents who select regular MPS schools). The results indicate that Chapter 220 parents are half as less likely as the reference category to possess information on the principal or to gather information on all the characteristics they deem important in selecting a school.

CHAPTER 5. *Shopping for Schools*

1. Cleveland uses the term *scholarship* to refer to the publicly financed vouchers they provide to parents. A random survey was conducted with 1,014 scholarship recipients and 1,006 applicants who did not enroll in the program after receiving a scholarship.

2. The Public Policy Forum was unable to obtain a list of parents participating in the Milwaukee School Choice Program because our FOIA request to DPI was denied. For this reason, the only information we have about the parents in the voucher program is from parents' calls to the Forum. In the end a full analysis of the voucher program needs to conduct a systematic survey of voucher parents. Current studies are clearly limited because the state will not publicly release this information.

3. We had visited many of these schools ourselves and had formed impressions regarding the level of information provided by schools. To combat any biases that we as researchers had obtained over the course of five years of studying voucher schools, we felt it was imperative that we select parent-visitors that were not well informed about the voucher program. Therefore our major criterion was their interest in searching for a school. We shared none of our prior experiences with the parent-researchers and only discussed their experiences after all visits had been made and all forms collected.

4. All of our parent-researchers were female. Five were parents of school-aged children. The two who were not parents examined schools by focusing their questions on a friend's child and a niece, respectively. Three of the interviewers were African American, two were foreign students, and two were non-Hispanic whites. Five of the seven researchers were residents of the City of Milwaukee. The team of seven parent-researchers was led by Tatyana Karaman with the assistance of Maria Spirova, Darlene Budd, Elizabeth Clark, Julie Siegel, Yaasmeen Joseph, and Berthina Joseph. Their work was invaluable to this project and we thank them for their assistance.

5. We would like to thank Mark Schneider for generously sharing his interview protocol with us.

6. In July 1999 the Forum released its first poster-sized directory of all the schools participating in MPCP along with the basic data we obtained in our annual census of voucher schools. Though quite limited, this is the only source of basic information on voucher schools. We printed thousands of copies of these posters and distributed them primarily at the public libraries. We updated the information for 2000 and released a second poster in May 2000. In January 2001 we printed our third updated poster. We know because of the wide distribution of these posters and our discussions with choice school administrators that voucher schools have come to rely on the poster as a way of marketing their schools.

7. Teske et al. 2000 conducted parent visits in order to compare how consumer-friendly charter schools were versus traditional public schools. They found that charter schools were far more responsive to requests by parents for information than public schools.

8. Information for voucher schools was obtained from our annual census of private voucher schools. Information on public schools was obtained from a booklet sent annually to all parents in Milwaukee during the public school selection period. This booklet, called *Directions,* provides information on all public elementary, middle, and high schools in Milwaukee.

9. Data on Milwaukee public schools and charter schools are available from several sources both online and in print. The accountability book provides several pages' worth of data from enrollment to student demographics, teacher stability, and student assessment data. (See *http://www.milwaukee. k12.wi.us/*) In addition to this large report a smaller report is sent annually to all parents in Milwaukee when the school selection period is approaching. This booklet, called *Directions,* provides information on all elementary, middle, and high schools.

10. Information could be obtained either verbally or in written form. Of the forty-one schools we visited, twenty-four provided written materials on the school.

11. The range in the amount of information provided and in the parent-researchers' feelings about making a choice was just as broad for the public schools visited as for the choice schools. Parents' schooling decisions, however, are not the sole means of accountability for public schools in Milwaukee.

CHAPTER 6. *Do the Dollars Follow the Child?*

1. In all three years of our financial impact analyses we focus only on state aid and do not attempt to analyze the impact of the choice program on school districts' tax levies. We do so because a district may have statutory authority to levy up to a certain limit but may choose not to maximize that authority for political reasons.

2. For example, in the 1997–99 biennial budget DPI reestimated the cost of the voucher program (because of the injunction forbidding expansion of the program to religious schools) and requested $20.4 million less in general purpose revenue than the previous budget's base amount. After the Wisconsin Supreme Court ruling allowing the expansion, DPI requested general purpose revenue totaling $80.6 million to fund the program in the 1999–2001 biennial budget. For the 2001–03 biennial budget DPI requested $133.8 million in general purpose revenue, a $34.3-million increase over the previous budget's base.

3. The Legislative Audit Bureau later confirmed our findings that MPS received "extra" equalization aid because the the voucher payment was calculated simultaneously with the equalization aid calculation. The bureau found, however, that the "extra" aid did not cover the total cost of the voucher payment. Wisconsin Legislative Audit Bureau, "An Evaluation: Milwaukee Parental Choice Program," Audit No. 00–2 (Madison: Legislative Audit Bureau, February 2000), Appendix V.

4. The averages reflect all school districts except MPS, which is treated separately, and the Norris and Salem #7 districts, which did not receive any state general aid in 1999–2000.

5. The Norris and Trevor School Districts are not included in this analysis because they did not receive state general aid in 2000–01.

6. The amendment also required voucher schools to administer the state third grade reading comprehension exam. None of these changes to the program ultimately survived the budget process.

7. Memo to Wisconsin legislature from Bob Lang, Legislative Fiscal Bureau Director, "Funding for the Milwaukee Parental Choice Program," May 8, 2001. Our own analysis found a statistically significant correlation of −.469 between the percent change in a district's property value from 1997 to 1999 and a district's percent change in state aid from 1998 to 2000. No statistically significant relationship exists between a district's change in state aid and the amount subtracted from a district's aid for the voucher payment.

8. The voucher amount when the interviews were conducted was approximately $5,100 per full-time student. The tuition rates at these voucher schools are much lower than that voucher amount. Only three of the ninety-one schools participating in 1999–2000 charge higher tuition than the voucher amount.

9. Learning Enterprise Institute and Grandview High School are partnership schools.

10. We calculate this figure by using 1998–99 data to compare the percentage of total estimated revenue from vouchers versus the percentage of student body that receives vouchers.

11. This total includes only permits in which the occupancy of the building was designated as school, day care, or mixed use and where the permit was obtained sometime after the school joined the choice program.

12. The third category in which we found a bulk of permits was air conditioning and heating work, for which there were sixteen permits totaling $1,236,745 in estimated costs.

13. The repayment to the state is not due until the end of the school year. Schools may therefore earn interest income on the overpayment.

14. The table represents data from all schools, but schools with several campuses, such as St. Vincent Pallotti or Seeds of Health, are combined.

CHAPTER 7. *Choice School Accountability: A Consensus of Views*

1. The panel was chaired by Mary P. Hoy, who at the time of this study was the dean of the School of Education at Marquette University, and William Harvey, who at the time of this study was dean of the School of Education at the University of Wisconsin-Milwaukee. Members of the panel included Michele Foster, Claremont Graduate School; Paul T. Hill, University of Washington; Mary Huba, Iowa State University; William Morgan, Cleveland State University; S. E. Phillips, Michigan State University; and Amy Stuart Wells, University of California, Los Angeles. We are indebted to our panel members for their advice and their oversight of this study. The conclusions presented are those of the authors alone.

2. School administrators include principals, assistant principals, headmasters, and business managers as well as other individuals holding various titles who have a role in the day-to-day management of schools. At the outset of this study we intended to have students play a major role as stakeholders in this study. At the time of the study, however, all of the choice participants in Cleveland were between kindergarten and third grade, and in Milwaukee the majority of participants were below the fifth grade. For this reason, we did not interview students.

3. We define taxpayers as anyone over the age of seventeen who resides in Ohio or Wisconsin. We specifically asked in the survey to speak with the adult who had celebrated the most recent birthday and asked them to answer from a taxpayer perspective.

4. The five Cleveland public schools were Anton Grdina Elementary, Central Middle School, Newton D. Baker, South High School, and Tremont Elementary. The Cleveland private choice schools were Hope Central Academy, Hope Ohio City Academy, Mt. Pleasant Elementary, Saint Adalbert, and Saint Thomas/Saint Phillip. The public schools in Milwaukee were 53d St. Elementary, Curtin Elementary, Juneau High School, Maryland Avenue Elementary, and Parkview Elementary. The five private choice schools in Milwaukee were Bruce Guadalupe, Harambee, Learning Enterprise Institute of Wisconsin, Urban Day, and Woodlands Elementary. At the time the interviews were conducted religious schools did not participate in Milwaukee. In Cleveland religious schools were participating, so we conducted interviews with parents who sent their children to religious and to nonreligious private schools. We contacted the administrators and five teachers affiliated with each of these schools. We conducted ten parent interviews from each school. In order to ensure a broader sample of parents, we also interviewed parents at a school expo in Milwaukee. In addition, we interviewed a randomly selected group of parents from those that applied to the Cleveland Scholarship Program.

5. Cleveland Public Schools serves approximately 70,000 students, MPS

approximately 103,000 students. These school districts have many factors in common. Both serve large urban areas with high levels of children who live in poverty. More than 40 percent of the children in Cleveland live in poverty, and 38 percent of the children in Milwaukee live in poverty (1990 Census). Of those children that attend MPS, approximately 66 percent are eligible for free or reduced-price lunch. In both school districts, approximately 60 percent of the student body is African American, 5 percent Asian, and 12 percent Hispanic.

6. Our interviewers were students at the University of Wisconsin-Milwaukee (UWM) and Cleveland State University (CSU). They were chosen on the basis of their previous interviewing experience and understanding of social science research methods. The interviewers went through a training session conducted by the staff of the Public Policy Forum. In addition, the interviewers were provided with information on the school choice program in the respective cities. The interviews were not tape recorded. The interviewer was required to write down the responses made by the interviewee and then entered the responses into a password encoded database on the Internet. This method of data entry ensured almost immediate access to the interview data. The team at CSU was directed by Ann Thornton with the assistance of Tyree Ayers, Ronnie Dunn, Margaret Gerba, and Tobey Manns. The UWM interviewers were Jackie Champagne, Audra Grant, Jolene Jesse, Ann Lorman, Dayna Velasco, and Emily Van Dunk.

7. The categorization of these data involved taking hundreds of responses and breaking each down into what can be termed databits. These databits are the phrases or words within the response that can be grouped into categories. Two levels of categorization took place. First, each response was broken into phrases and words. The next step involved taking these phrases and grouping them into the final categories that we labeled school program, school characteristics, teachers, general outcomes, test score outcomes, safety/discipline, parental involvement, reputation, and school characteristics. In order to clarify this process we include the following example:

A public school parent responded to Question 1: *"Two of my children are special needs kids and it is important to me that I find a program that works for my kids. I believe each child is different and that no one school will work for every child. One of my children needed traditional schools and the other did not. The method of teaching is important to me and it is important to understand if your child will fit into that program. I am very interested in the style of teaching because each child learns differently."* From this response we extracted the following databits: (1) focus of the school, i.e., traditional; (2) meeting individual needs of children; (3) method of teaching. These three databits were sorted into the following categories: focus of school, i.e., traditional = *School Program;* method of teaching = *School Program;* meeting individual needs = *Outcomes General.* The final coding for this parent would include the factors *School Program* and

Outcomes General. While the parent mentioned two *School Program* databits, we are looking at the percentage of respondents who mentioned a particular category, not the number of responses for each category. We believe that in this way we are not overweighting particular categories.

The final categories include the following databits: *School Program:* method of teaching, course offerings, bilingual offerings, multicultural curriculum, challenging curriculum, foreign language offerings, hands-on learning, innovative teaching, job preparation courses, mission and philosophy of school, focus of the school, advanced course offerings, special needs course offerings, expectations of school program, field trip offerings, honors program offerings; *Teachers:* character of teachers, educational degrees of teachers, gender of teachers, how the teachers treat the children, qualifications and experience of teachers, race/ethnicity of teachers, retention rate of teachers, accountability of teachers for student learning, teachers' moral values, ability of the teacher to motivate students, the certification of teachers, and the staff development opportunities for teachers; *Outcomes General:* development of cognitive skills, development of creative skills, development of lifetime skills, grade point average, graduation rate from high school, amount of homework, meeting individual needs of child, grade advancement, study habits school encourages, the grading process, where alumni end up, is my child learning?, do my kids like it?; *Outcomes Test Scores:* standardized test scores; *School Characteristics:* atmosphere of the school, attendance rate, attrition rate of students, classroom size, makeup of student body, history of school, cultural diversity of school, number of students, student/teacher ratio, ratio of teachers to assistants; *Safety and Discipline:* amount of violence in schools, appearance of outside community, code of discipline, security procedures in place at school, level of disciplinary actions; *Reputation of School:* recommendations of teachers and other parents, reputation of the school, does the school rank as one of the best?; *Parent Involvement:* ability to go in and talk with teacher, open communication between parent and teacher, how involved parents are with the school, parental satisfaction, requirements for parental involvement, if training is offered for parents, can parents work with school to improve it?, what committees are run by parents?

8. We contracted Lein/Spiegelhoff, Inc., a survey research company in Brookfield, Wisconsin, to interview residents in Ohio and Wisconsin. We sampled the adult in a household who "celebrated the most recent birthday." If the person was not available, a callback was setup. Three callbacks were conducted. We first conducted a random digit dialing with no oversampling for race. This gave us a sample with 7.21 percent African Americans in Ohio and 2.23 percent African Americans in Wisconsin. Our oversample resulted in 12.5 percent African Americans in each state. To obtain 771 interviews required 6,244 telephone numbers. Approximately 20 percent of the attempts resulted in a refusal; other interviews were not completed because the interviewer reached an answering

machine or voice mail, nonworking or disconnected number, a busy signal, fax machine, a business number, or government number.

9. The effect of weighting the African American responses was less than 0.1 percent. For this reason, we report the unweighted frequencies in the tables.

10. If the interviewee asked, then the following definitions of mandatory and voluntary were read: "Mandatory"—must be reported by a private school participating in a school choice program. "Voluntary"—up to the individual schools participating in a school choice program to report. The survey respondent was also given the option of saying "Don't Know."

11. We ran difference of means tests for each question. We report only those differences that were statistically significant at the .05 level of probability. Our income group contained three categories, low, medium, and high. Low is defined as households with less than $24,999 in annual income ($N = 174$), middle income is defined as those households between $25,000 and 60,000 in annual income ($N = 362$), and high is defined as those households with greater than $60,000 in annual household income ($N = 120$). Less than 3.4 percent of those surveyed chose a racial or ethnic category other than white or African American. Because this small sample size makes it impossible to examine group differences, we group this 3.4 percent with white for purposes of analysis. We ran the frequencies by excluding this 3.4 percent but did not see any significant changes in the frequencies. Because we did not want to lose data by selecting out these 3.4 percent, the white category includes this other non–African American category.

12. We used responses to Question 9 on our survey to measure support or opposition to school choice.

13. Order is alphabetical and does not indicate importance.

14. According to the archdiocese of Milwaukee website (*www.archmil.org*), grades eight and four took the Wisconsin standardized exams in 2002.

15. In the 1993, 1997, and 2001 state elections for state superintendent of public instruction in Wisconsin the candidate supported by groups opposed to school choice won election. The result has been a lasting perception that this state agency is biased against choice.

References

Adler, Jonathon H. 1996. Rent seeking behind the green curtain. *Regulation: The Review of Business and Government* 19(4). Washington, D.C.: Cato Institute.

Anyon, Jean. 1997. *Ghetto Schooling: A Political Economy of Urban Educational Reform.* New York: Teachers College Press.

Armour, David J., and Brett M. Peiser. 1997. Competition in education: Interdistrict choice in Massachusetts. Paper presented at Conference on Rethinking School Governance, at the Kennedy School of Government, Harvard University, June, Cambridge.

———. 1998. Interdistrict choice in Massachusetts. In *Learning from School Choice,* ed. Paul E. Peterson and Bryan C. Hassel. Washington, D.C.: Brookings Institution Press.

Ball, Stephen J., Richard Bowe, and Sharon Gewirtz. 1994. Competitive schooling: Values, ethics and cultural engineering. *Journal of Curriculum and Supervision* 9(4):350–67.

Barnow, Burt S., Glen G. Cain, and Arthur S. Goldberger. 1980. Issues in the analysis of selectivity bias. In *Evaluation Studies Review Annual,* Vol. 5, ed. Ernst W. Stromsdorfer and George Farkas. Beverly Hills: Sage Publications.

Bierlein, L. A. 1996. *Charter Schools: Initial Findings.* Baton Rouge: Louisiana Education Policy Research Center.

Bonotti, Sally, Rick Ginsburg, and Brian Cobb. 1999. Teachers in charter schools and traditional schools: A comparative study. *Education Policy Analysis Archives* 7(22).

Buttolph-Johnson, Janet, and Richard A. Joshlyn. 1995. *Political Science Research Methods,* 3d ed. Washington, D.C.: CQ Press.

Carl, Jim. 1996. Unusual allies: Elite and grass-roots origins of parental choice in Milwaukee. *Teachers College Record* 98:266–85.

Carver, Rebecca L., and Laura H. Salganik. 1991. You can't have choice without information. *Equity and Choice* (Spring):41–75.

Chubb, John, and Terry Moe. 1990. *Politics, Markets, and America's Schools.* Washington, D.C.: Brookings Institution Press.

Damaris, Alfred. 1992. *Logit Modeling: Practical Applications.* Quantitative Applications in the Social Sciences Series no. 86. Newbury Park, Calif.: Sage Publications.

Darling-Hammond, Linda, and Carol Ascher. 1991. *Creating Accountability in Big City Schools.* New York: National Center for Restructuring Education, Schools, and Teaching.

Dee, Thomas S. 1998. Competition and the quality of public schools. *Economics of Education Review* 17(4):419–27.

Delli Carpini, Michael X., and Scott Keeter. 1996. *What Americans Know about Politics and Why It Matters.* New Haven: Yale University Press.

Du Bois, W. E. B. 1973. *The Education of Black People: Ten Critiques, 1906– 1960.* Ed. Herbert Aptheker. New York: Monthly Review Press.

Egen, Rachel, Dwight Holmes, and Elliot Mincberg. 2000. *The 40 Percent Surcharge: How Taxpayers Overpay for Milwaukee's Private School Voucher Program.* Washington, D.C.: People for the American Way.

Friedman, Milton. 1962. *Capitalism and Freedom.* Chicago: University of Chicago Press.

Fuller, Howard, and George Mitchell. 1999. The fiscal impact of school choice on the Milwaukee public schools. *Current Education Issues* 99(2). Milwaukee: Marquette University Institute for the Transformation of Learning.

Geller, Christopher R., David L. Sjoquist, and Mary Beth Walker. 2001. *The Effect of Private School Competition on Public School Performance.* Occasional Paper no. 15. New York: Teachers College, Columbia University.

Glass, Gene V., and D. A. Mathews. 1991. Are data enough? Review of *Politics, Markets, and America's Schools. Educational Researcher* 20:24–27.

Glass, Sandra R. 1997. Markets and myths: Autonomy in public and private schools. *Education Policy Analysis Archives* 5(1).

Gorard, Stephen. 1997. *School Choice in an Established Market.* Aldershot, England: Ashgate Publishing.

Greene, Jay P., William G. Howell, and Paul E. Peterson. 1997. An evaluation of the Cleveland Scholarship Program. Paper presented at Program on Education Policy and Governance, at the Kennedy School of Government, Harvard University, June, Cambridge.

Greene, Jay P., Paul E. Peterson, and Jiangtao Du. 1997. *The Effectiveness of School Choice: The Milwaukee Experiment.* Harvard University Education Policy and Governance Occasional Paper no. 1. Cambridge: Harvard University.

———. 1999. Effectiveness of school choice: The Milwaukee experiment. *Education and Urban Society* 31(2):190–213.

Hamilton, Scott W. 2000. Accountability in a world of charter and vouchers: Are market forces enough? Paper presented at Conference on Vouchers, Charters and Public Education, at the Program on Education Policy and Governance, Harvard University, 9–10 March, Cambridge.

Hassel, Bryan. 1998. Governance and educational equality. In *Learning from School Choice,* ed. Paul E. Peterson and Bryan C. Hassel. Washington, D.C.: Brookings Institution Press.

Hatcher, L. 1994. *A Step-by-Step Approach to Using SASo System for Factor Analysis and Structural Equation Modeling.* Cary, N.C.: SAS Institute.

Heckman, James J. 1980. Sample selection bias as a specification error. In *Evaluation Studies Review Annual,* Vol. 5., ed. Ernst W. Stromsdorfer and George Farkas. Beverly Hills: Sage Publications.

Henig, Jeffrey R. 1994. *Rethinking School Choice: Limits of the Market Metaphor.* Princeton: Princeton University Press.

———. 1996. The local dynamics of choice: Ethnic preferences and institutional responses. In *Who Chooses? Who Loses? Culture, Institutions, and the Unequal Effects of School Choice,* ed. Bruce Fuller, Richard F. Elmore, and Gary Orfield. New York: Teachers College Press.

———. 1999. School choice outcomes. In *School Choice and Social Controversy: Politics, Policy, and Law,* ed. Stephen D. Sugarman and Frank R. Kemerer. Washington, D.C.: Brookings Institution Press.

Henry, Gary T. 1996. Community accountability: A theory of information, accountability, and school improvement. *Phi Delta Kap-
pan* 78(1):85–90.

Henry, Gary T., Kent C. Dickey, and Janet C. Areson. 1991. Stakeholder
participation in educational performance monitoring systems.
Educational Evaluation and Policy Analysis 13:177–88.

Hess, Frederick M. 2000. Hints of the pick-axe: The impact of competition on public schooling in Milwaukee. Paper presented at annual meeting of the American Educational Research Association, 24–28 April, New Orleans.

Hess, Frederick M., Robert Maranto, and Scott Milliman. 2000. Can
markets set bureaucrats free? The effects of school choice on
teacher empowerment in the public schools. Paper presented at
annual meeting of the American Educational Research Association, 24–28 April, New Orleans.

Hill, Paul T. 1996. *School-Centered Reform and Accountability*. Seattle:
University of Washington Press.

Hill, Paul T., Christine Campbell, and James Harvey. 2000. *It Takes a
City: Getting Serious about Urban School Reform*. Washington,
D.C.: Brookings Institution Press.

Hill, Paul T., and Mary Beth Celio. 1998. *Fixing Urban Schools*. Washington, D.C.: Brookings Institution Press.

Hosmer, David W., and Stanley Lemeshow. 1989. *Applied Logistic Regression*. New York: John Wiley and Sons.

Hoxby, Caroline M. 1994. *Do Private Schools Provide Competition for
Public Schools?* Working Paper no. W4978. Washington, D.C.:
National Bureau of Economic Research.

———. 1998. Analyzing school choice reforms that use America's traditional forms of parental choice. In *Learning from School Choice*,
ed. Paul E. Peterson and Bryan C. Hassel. Washington, D.C.:
Brookings Institution Press.

———. 1999. The effects of school choice on curriculum and atmosphere. In *Earning and Learning: How Schools Matter*, ed. Susan
Mayer and Paul E. Peterson. Washington, D.C.: Brookings Institution Press.

———. 2003. School choice productivity: Could school choice be a tide
that lifts all boats? In *The Economics of School Choice*, ed. Caroline M. Hoxby. Chicago: University of Chicago Press.

————. 2002. The cost of accountability. Available at http://post. economics.harvard.edu/faculty/hoxby/papers/costofac.pdf.

Howell, William G., and Paul E. Peterson. 2002. *The Education Gap: Vouchers and Urban Schools.* Washington, D.C.: Brookings Institution Press.

Institute for Wisconsin's Future. 1999. Draft response to the Public Policy Forum report. Milwaukee: Institute for Wisconsin's Future. Unpublished.

Kemerer, Frank R. 1999. School choice accountability. In *School Choice and Social Controversy: Politics, Policy, and Law,* ed. Stephen D. Sugarman and Frank R. Kemerer. Washington, D.C.: Brookings Institution Press.

Levin, Henry M. 1998. Educational vouchers: Effectiveness, choice, and costs. *Journal of Policy Analysis and Management* 17:373–92.

Lupia, Arthur, and Mathew McCubbins. 1998. *The Democratic Dilemma: Can Citizens Learn What They Need to Know?* New York: Cambridge University Press.

Manna, Paul F. 1999. How parents make decisions and send signals when they choose their children's schools. Paper presented at annual meeting of the Midwest Political Science Association, 15–17 April, Chicago.

Manski, Charles F. 1992. Education vouchers and social mobility. *Economics of Education Review* 11(4):351–69.

Maynard, Rebecca A., Lauren Scher, Elliot Weinbaum, Connie Keefe, and Andrew Sparks. 2002. School Choice in Philadelphia. Paper presented at annual meeting of the American Educational Research Association, 1–6 April, New Orleans.

Maxwell, Joseph Alex. 1996. *Qualitative Research Design: An Interactive Approach.* Newbury Park, Calif.: Sage Publications.

McEwan, Patrick J. 2000. The potential impact of large-scale voucher programs. *Review of Educational Research* 70(2):103–49.

McGuinn, Patrick, and Frederick M. Hess. 2000. Business as usual: The minimal competitive effects of the Cleveland voucher program. Paper presented at annual meeting of the American Educational Research Association, 24–28 April, New Orleans.

Mead, Julie. 2000. *Publicly Funded School Choice Options in Milwaukee: An Examination of the Legal Issues.* Milwaukee: Public Policy Forum.

Metcalf, Kim K. 1998. *A Comparative Evaluation of the Cleveland Scholarship and Tutoring Grant Program Year One: 1996–1997.* Bloomington: Indiana University School of Education and the Junior Achievement Evaluation Project, Smith Research Center.

Metcalf, Kim K., Patricia Muller, William Boone, Polly Tait, Frances Stuge, and Nicole Stacey. 1998. *Evaluation of the Cleveland scholarship program: Second-year report (1997–98).* Bloomington: Indiana Center for Evaluation.

———. 1999. *Evaluation of the Cleveland Scholarship and Tutoring Grant Program, 1996–1999.* Bloomington: Indiana Center for Evaluation.

Mintrom, Michael, and David N. Plank. 2000. The emerging market for schooling: Evidence from Michigan. Paper presented at Conference on Vouchers, Charters, and Public Education, at the Program on Education Policy and Governance, Harvard University, 9–10 March, Cambridge.

Mitchell, Susan. 1996. Why choice supporters can't relax. *Wisconsin Interest* 5(1).

Moe, Terry M., ed. 1995. *Private Vouchers.* Stanford: Hoover Institution Press.

———. 2001. *Schools, Vouchers, and the American Public.* Washington, D.C.: Brookings Institution Press.

Nelson, F. Howard, Rachel Egen, and Dwight Holmes. 2001. Revenues, expenditures and taxpayer subsidies in Milwaukee's voucher schools. Paper presented at annual meeting of the American Education Finance Association, March, Cincinnati.

Nunnaly, J. 1978. *Psychometric Theory.* New York: McGraw-Hill.

Oakes, J. 1986. *Educational Indicators: A Guide for Policymakers.* New Brunswick, N.J.: Center for Policy Research in Education.

People for the American Way Foundation. 2002. *A Painful Price: How the Milwaukee Voucher Surcharge Undercuts Wisconsin's Education Priorities.* Washington, D.C.: People for the American Way.

Peterson, Paul E., William G. Howell, and Jay P. Greene. *An Evaluation of the Cleveland Voucher Program after Two Years.* Cambridge: Program on Education Policy and Governance, Harvard University.

Public Agenda. 1999. *On Thin Ice: How Advocates and Opponents Could Misread the Public's Views on Vouchers and Charter Schools.* New York: Public Agenda.

Public Policy Forum. 1999. More choice for parents has not reduced MPS aid. *In Fact* 87(3). Milwaukee: Public Policy Forum.

———. 2000. School finance laws mute competition. *Research Brief* 88(10). Milwaukee: Public Policy Forum.

Rofes, Eric. 1998. *How Are School Districts Responding to Charter Laws and Charter Schools?* Berkeley: Policy Analysis for California Education.

Rouse, Cecilia Elena. 1998. Private school vouchers and student achievement: An evaluation of the Milwaukee Parental Choice Program. *Quarterly Journal of Economics* 113:553.

———. 1998. *Schools and Student Achievement: More Evidence from the Milwaukee Parental Choice Program.* Princeton: Princeton University and National Bureau for Economic Research.

Schneider, Mark, Paul Teske, and Melissa Marshall. 2000. *Choosing Schools: Consumer Choice and the Quality of American Schools.* Princeton: Princeton University Press.

Schneider, Mark, Paul Teske, Melissa Marshall, and Christine Roch. 1998. Shopping for schools: In the land of the blind, the one-eyed parent may be enough. *American Journal of Political Science* 42:769–93.

———. 1999. Heuristics, low information rationality, and choosing public goods: Broken windows as shortcuts to information about school performance. *Urban Affairs Review* 34:729–41.

Smith, Kevin B., and Kenneth J. Meier. 1995. *The Case Against School Choice: Politics, Markets, and Fools.* Armonk, N.Y.: M. E. Sharpe.

Stuart-Wells, Amy. 1993. *Time to Choose: America at the Crossroads of School Choice Policy.* New York: Hill and Wang.

Teske, Paul, Mark Schneider, Jack Buckley, and Sara Clark. 2000. The effect of charter school competition on public schools in five cities. Paper presented at annual meeting of the Midwest Political Science Association, 27–30 April, Chicago.

———. 2000. *Does Charter School Competition Improve Traditional Public Schools?* Civic Report no. 10. New York: Center for Civic Innovation at the Manhattan Institute.

Thompson, Bruce. 1998. The MPS budget and school choice. Available at http://www.execpc.com/~brt/myths.htm.

Toulmin, Charlie. 1999. Memo to John Kalwitz, City of Milwaukee Common Council President. 22 March.

Van Dunk, Emily. 1998. *Parental Involvement and School Choice: A Look at Private School Choice in Cleveland and Milwaukee.* Milwaukee: Public Policy Forum.

———. 1998. Seeing through the rhetoric: Views on school choice from parents, educators and elected officials in Cleveland and Milwaukee. Paper presented at annual meeting of the Midwest Political Science Association, 23–25 April, Chicago.

———. 2000. Education. In *Crane and Hagensick's Wisconsin Government and Politics,* 7th ed., ed. Ronald E. Weber. New York: McGraw-Hill.

———. 2001. Education consumers: A comparative look at the competitive effects of school choice policy. Paper presented at annual meeting of the American Political Science Association, 29 August–2 September, San Francisco.

———. 2001. Choice parents and choice school administrators: What they can tell us about the impacts of vouchers. Paper presented at annual meeting of the Western Political Science Association, 15–18 March, Las Vegas.

Van Dunk, Emily, David Meissner, and Jeffrey Browne. 1998. *Choice School Accountability: A Consensus of Views in Ohio and Wisconsin.* Milwaukee: Public Policy Forum.

Wells, Amy Stuart. 1998. Beyond the rhetoric of charter school reform: A study of ten California school districts. *UCLA Charter School Study.* Los Angeles: University of California.

Williams, Annette Polly. 1994. Choice debate is about who controls education. *National Minority Politics* (January):7.

Wilson, James Q., and George L. Kelling. 1982. The police and neighborhood safety. *The Atlantic* (March):29–38.

Wilson, Steven F. 1992. *Reinventing the Schools: A Radical Plan for Boston.* Boston: Pioneer Institute.

Wisconsin Legislative Fiscal Bureau. 1999. *Milwaukee Parental Choice Program.* Informational Paper no. 29. Madison: Legislative Fiscal Bureau.

Witte, John F. 1995. *Fifth Year Report: Milwaukee Parental Choice Pro-*

gram. Madison: University of Wisconsin Department of Political Science and the Robert M. La Follette Institute of Public Affairs.

———. 2000. *The Market Approach to Education: An Analysis of America's First Voucher Program.* Princeton: Princeton University Press.

Witte, John F., Christopher A. Thorn, Kim M. Pritchard, and Michele Claibourn. 1994. *Fourth Year Report: Milwaukee Parental Choice Program.* Madison: University of Wisconsin Department of Political Science and the Robert M. La Follette Institute of Public Affairs.

Worthen, Blaine R., and James R. Sanders. 1987. *Educational Evaluation: Alternative Approaches and Practical Guidelines.* New York: Longman.

Index

accountability, 2, 3, 75–77, 94, 95; guidelines for, 169–76, 187–89; information and, 115; market; principles and, 33–44; parental visits to schools and, 99; power of school choice and, 178–90; school success/failure and, 142, 145–46, 168

accreditation, 22, 163, 164, 165, 166, 175

ACT college placement exam, 10

advanced placement tests, 10

African Americans, 13, 162, 168; accountability guidelines and, 170, 171, 174; parents, 10–11, 12; students, 6–7, 11, 84, 85, 194n21; taxpayer surveys and, 151, 152, 153, 154; teachers, 49

after-school enrichment programs, 142

Agape Center of Academic Excellence, 37

aggregate mobility rate, 43

Ahmuty, Chris, 17–18

Alticor, Inc., 5

Alum Rock project, 105–6

American Civil Liberties Union, 17

American Education Reform Foundation, 17

Arizona, 7, 47

Armour, David J., 47

Asian students, 11

attendance zones, 4

Believers in Christ Christian Academy, 37

bilingual education, 126

Black Alliance for Educational Options (BAEO), 2, 10

Blessed Sacrament School, 144

Blessed Trinity Catholic School, 33, 34, 35, 36, 37

Blyden Delany Academy, 141, 144

"broken window" theory, 111

Bruce Guadalupe School, 25, 35, 202n4

budgets, 15, 17, 26, 200n2

bureaucracy, 2

Bush, George W., 1

busing, 62

California, 5, 105–6

Carl, Jim, 12

Catholic East Elementary School, 140, 144

Catholic schools, 24, 26, 135, 139

CEO America, 2

Ceria M. Travis Academy, 141

Chapter 220 program, 11, 77, 78, 82, 198n23; number of students in, 80; parental choice and, 92–93; parents' access to information and, 87, 89; parent survey and, 84, 85, 86

charter schools, 11, 24, 52, 100, 192n3, 195n3; competition and, 7, 48; environment of, 112; number of Milwaukee students in, 80; researcher visits to, 100; teachers and, 51, 57

child psychologists, 139

Chubb, John, 1, 5, 50, 75, 175

church attendance, 87–90, 93, 94, 95, 197n17
Chvala, Chuck, 129
city schools, 77
class size, 91, 98, 156, 174, 204n7
Cleveland, 4, 7, 47, 155–56, 176; parent volunteer program in, 170; public schools in, 202n4; scholarships (vouchers) in, 98, 149–50, 171, 199n1
Common Council of the City of Milwaukee, 24
Community Vision Academy, 141
competition, 2–3, 4, 146; competitive presence, 59–60, 62, 63, 64, 68, 71; funding and, 130–31; hypotheses about effects of, 50–54; legislation and, 133, 168; parental accountability and, 6, 23; productivity and, 7; response of public schools to, 46–47; school changes and, 59–73; school closures and, 26; student achievement and, 46; weakness of, 180. See also free market principles
computers, 139
conservatives, 12, 13
"controlled choice," 79
Corpus Christi School, 144
Council for American Private Education (CAPE), 2
court records, 138–39
criminal charges, 26, 27, 28
Cronbach's alpha, 54, 55, 56, 192n4
curriculum, 159, 160, 173, 187; information provided by schools, 116, 117; parental school visits and, 99, 111, 116, 117

decentralization, 61
Dee, Thomas S., 47
desegregation, 78
DeVos, Dick, 5
discipline, 91, 98, 103, 116, 157, 204n7
Divine Savior Holy Angels High School, 31, 38
Downtown Montessori (school), 25
Draper, Timothy, 5
dropouts, 1, 27

Early View Academy of Excellence, 30, 31, 32, 36, 37, 144
elections (2000), 5
elementary schools, 61, 70, 136, 150
Empowering Parents through Informed Choices in Education (EPIC), 105
enrollment, 3, 7, 9, 126; changes in, 61, 65; competition effects on, 58; free-market accountability and, 29–33; full-time equivalent (FTE), 8; history of Milwaukee program and, 23–24; increase in, 15, 183; number of voucher students and, 30–33; open, 11, 75, 195n3; percentage of voucher students, 146; periods of, 23; ratio of overall and voucher enrollment, 103, 104
entrepreneurs, 6
equalization aid, 122–23, 127, 128, 129, 201n3
exams, standardized, 18
Exito Education Center, 25, 27–28
expenditures (dollar amounts), 9–10
extracurricular activities, 91

Family Academy Inc., 144
financial aid, 102, 103, 116, 117
financial audits, 161, 173
free market principles, 2, 3, 12, 22; accountability and, 121–22, 181–82; consumer demand and, 4; government subsidy and, 142–43, 145; supply and demand, 33–44. See also competition
Friedman, Milton, 4–5
Fuller, Howard, 10–11, 124, 131
full-time equivalent (FTE) students, 80, 104, 124

Geller, Christopher R., 47
Gorard, Stephen, 47
Gospel Lutheran School, 140, 144
Grace Christian School, 25, 28
grade level, 39–40, 61, 103, 193n15; competitive effects and, 65; education costs and, 126; parent surveys and, 82; reading comprehension and, 85; teacher work-lives and, 67; WKCE and, 69, 70
graduate placement, 161, 162
graduation rates, 99, 161, 173, 187

graffiti, 102, 111, 112, 114
Grandview High School, 38, 201n9
Gray's Child Development Center, 141
Greene, Jay P., 98
Gregory B. Flood Sr. Christian Academy, 25, 28–29

Harambee Community School, 30, 31, 35, 141, 202n4; cumulative percent of voucher enrollment, 36; enrollment increase at, 32; number of voucher enrolled students, 34
Henig, Jeffrey R., 105
Hess, Frederick M., 7, 47
Highland Community School, 25
high schools, 40, 41, 44, 61, 65, 150
Hispanics, 11, 49
Holy Redeemer Christian Academy, 30, 31, 32, 34, 36
Hoxby, Caroline M., 7, 47, 174, 194n22

Immaculate Conception and St. Augustine (school), 25
income levels, 75, 87, 88, 93; information requirements and, 162, 167; knowledge about schools and, 97; scholarships (vouchers) and, 149–50; taxpayer surveys and, 152, 154
Individuals with Disabilities Education Act (IDEA), 172

Joint Center for Political and Economic Studies, 154
Joint Finance Committee (Wisconsin legislature), 15
Juanita Virgil Academy, 25, 26–27

Kelling, George L., 111
Khamit Institute (school), 25
kindergarten students, 39, 40, 125

Learning Enterprise High School, 31, 37, 38, 201n9
legislation, 16, 17, 132
Legislative Audit Bureau (Wisconsin), 9, 43, 196n10, 201n3

Legislative Fiscal Bureau (Wisconsin), 132
liberals, 12, 13
lotteries, 75, 150
Louis Tucker Academy, 140, 144
lunches, free and reduced-price, 11, 82, 84, 85, 203n5
Lutheran schools, 37, 135, 140, 141, 144
Lutheran Special School, 141

magnet schools (public), 75
Manna, Paul F., 76–77
Market Approach to Education, The (Witte), 8
Marquette University High School, 31, 38
Marva Collins Preparatory School, 30, 31, 141; cumulative percent of voucher enrollment, 36, 37; enrollment increase at, 32; number of voucher enrolled students, 34; school cost per pupil, 144
math test scores, 68, 70–71, 73
Matthews, John, 121
McCallum, Scott, 18
Medgar Evers Academy, 140, 144
Meier, Kenneth J., 47
Messmer High School, 30, 31; cumulative percent of voucher enrollment, 36, 37; enrollment increase at, 32; number of voucher enrolled students, 34; total enrollment and voucher students, 38
Messmer Preparatory Catholic School, 35, 37
Metropolitan Milwaukee Association of Commerce (MMAC), 12
Michigan, 5, 7
middle schools, 41, 61, 70, 178
Milwaukee, 4, 7, 21, 47, 101, 176; academic research panel and, 149; "broken windows" theory in, 111–15; competitive accountability theory in, 145–47; mayor of, 1, 134; parents of, 77; parent volunteer program in, 170; property values in, 11; school funding in, 123, 132; test scores in, 10; tuition costs in, 171; voucher funding in, 132; voucher program in, 3
Milwaukee Montessori School, 31

Milwaukee Multicultural Academy, 30, 32, 141

Milwaukee Parental Choice Program (MPCP), 7–8, 9, 17, 22; accountability and, 18; African-American parents and, 12; directory of participating schools, 199n6; enrollment increase and, 15; expansion of, 15–16, 50, 124, 134; funding of, 122–32; grade levels in, 40, 41, 61; history of, 23–29; legislative debates about, 121, 129; parent surveys and, 76; percentage of voucher students in, 42; private schools participating in, 60; voucher eligibility and, 191n2:2

Milwaukee Preparatory Academy, 25, 28

Milwaukee Public Schools (MPS), 7, 10, 19; charter schools and, 24; educational funding system and, 185, 186; enrollment, 9, 15; funding, 61, 123, 125–32, 133; intradistrict school choice, 78–79; parental choice and, 92, 93; parent surveys and, 81–82, 86–90; performance data of, 46; as poor district, 11; racial integration of, 78; response to competition, 183; school closures and, 27; teacher empowerment in, 54; teacher survey (2000), 48–50; test scores, 68, 69; three-choice selection process, 11, 77–79, 87; transportation services and, 195n5; voucher eligibility and, 14; voucher students previously enrolled in, 42, 43, 45. See also public school system

minorities, 11, 12, 78, 97, 192n3, 195n4

Mitchell, George, 124, 131

Mitchell, Susan, 17

Moe, Terry, 1, 5, 13, 154, 175; market short-comings and, 75; on public support for private school choice, 155; on student achievement, 50

Mother of Good Counsel (school), 31, 144

Mount Calvary Lutheran School, 37, 144

National Center for Education Statistics (NCES), 9

Nazareth Lutheran School, 144

Neighborhood House, 25, 28

neighborhoods, schools and, 111–15, 136

Neighborhood Schools Initiative (NSI), 62, 65

New York City, 6

nondiscrimination policies, 171–72

Norquist, John, 1, 134

North Milwaukee Christian School, 25, 28

Office of Management and Budget (federal agency), 14

Oklahoma Avenue Lutheran School, 140

O'Toole, Robert, 10, 124

Our Lady of Good Hope School, 144

Our Lady of Sorrows School, 140, 144

Our Lady Queen of Peace Parish, 140, 144

parents: accountability and, 2, 6, 18, 22, 170–71; choice of schools, 20; as consumers/shoppers, 52, 74–75, 97–99; demand for vouchers, 35, 38; desires of, 157–58; education marketplace and, 44–45; financial consequences of actions of, 167–68; history of Milwaukee program and, 23–29; informational needs of, 154–57, 183–84, 187; informed decision making of, 75–77, 82–90, 115–20; race of, 13, 88, 89, 90, 94, 95, 101; school choice and, 3–4, 5; school closures and, 29; signals in choice of, 90–94; student mobility rate and, 43; visits to schools, 99–103, 199n4

Parents Advancing Value in Education (PAVE), 125–26

Parklawn Christian School, 32, 141

partnership schools, 136

Peiser, Brett M., 47

Peterson, Paul E., 6

Pius XI High School, 31, 38

poverty level (federal standard), 150, 203n5

Prince of Peace/Principe de Paz (school), 25, 31, 34, 37

principals, 86–87, 89, 134, 139

private school choice, 1–3, 6–8; future funding of, 132–33; in Milwaukee, 8–18, 21; promise of, 3–6; state elections and, 205n15; taxpayer support for, 13; teachers' unions and, 60

private schools; church attendance by parents and, 89; competition with public schools, 12, 19; education market and, 74; enrollment by grade, 40–41; financial impacts on, 133–45; information gathering about, 163–67; money paid to, 9–10; number of Milwaukee students in, 79, 80; principals of, 86, 87; probationary period and, 176, 188; regulation of, 155; teachers and, 57, 172; voucher students previously enrolled in, 42, 43, 45. *See also* religious schools

proficiency levels, 1

property taxes, 122

Public Policy Forum, 3, 13, 23, 98, 134; parent-researchers and, 99–101, 105; parents' contact with, 178–80; school funding and, 125, 127, 128; public-private boards, 175, 188

public school system, 4, 6, 11, 46–47; competition and, 19, 50–51, 68–73, 133, 183; failure of, 13; financial impacts on, 123–32; impact of school choice on, 47–48; intradistrict school choice, 78–79; monopoly of education, 1; number of city children in, 42; parental visits to schools, 99; performance, 68–73; public funds and, 12; specialty and magnet schools, 74–75; student achievement and, 16, 148; teacher empowerment and, 51–52. *See also* Milwaukee Public Schools (MPS)

quality, accountability and, 39

racial integration, 78, 79

reading proficiency tests, 10, 68, 70, 71, 73

regulations, 148, 155

religious schools, 8, 12, 15, 23, 35, 41; in Cleveland, 150; expansion of MPCP and, 50, 124, 134; parent-researcher visits to, 106; scholarships and, 125. *See also* private schools

"rent-seekers," 143

Resurrection Catholic Academy, 37, 140, 144

Rofes, Eric, 47

role-based observation, 100

St. Adalbert School, 34, 36, 37

St. Alexander School, 144

St. Anthony's School, 30, 31, 32, 36, 140, 144

St. Barbara and Holy Spirit (school), 25

St. Bernadette School, 144

St. Catherine School, 37

St. Elizabeth Ann Seton Academy, 25

St. Gregory the Great (school), 31

St. Helen Grade School, 144

St. Joan Antida High School, 31, 37, 38

St. John Kanty School, 140, 144

St. Josaphat Parish School, 140, 144

St. Lawrence and St. Mathew (school), 25

St. Leo Catholic School/Urban Academy, 33, 34, 134, 141; cumulative percent of voucher enrollment, 36, 37; school cost per pupil, 144

St. Margaret Mary School, 31, 144

St. Martini Lutheran School, 37

St. Matthew School, 141

St. Paul Catholic School, 144

St. Peter Immanuel Lutheran School, 140, 144

St. Philip Neri Catholic School, 37

St. Rafael the Archangel (school), 25

St. Roman Parish School, 31

St. Rose Catholic Academy, 34, 36, 37, 141

St. Sebastian School, 31, 144

St. Veronica School, 31, 144

St. Vincent Pallotti School, 25, 144

Salam School, 30, 32, 37, 144

Schneider, Mark, 76, 81, 84; on parental choice, 97–98, 102; on school officials and information, 105

scholarships, in Cleveland, 125–26, 171

school boards, 74

schools: climate of, 53, 56; closures of, 2, 3, 24, 25, 26, 27–29; maintenance costs, 142; parental knowledge about, 19, 181; parent-researcher visits to, 105–15; productivity of, 7; safety at, 91, 98, 108, 113, 157, 204n7; shopping for, 96–99, 103–11, 184–85; size of, 23; success/failure of, 182, 186; top ten enrolling voucher students, 32, 34. *See also* elementary schools; high schools; middle schools; private schools; public school system; religious schools; *individual schools*

SER Benito Martinez Academy, 25, 27

Sherman Park Preschool, 141

Sinicki, Christine, 17

Smith, Kevin B., 47

social workers, 139

special education, 126

special programs, 58, 59

specialty schools (public), 75

student achievement, 50, 98, 116, 117, 148

students: aggregate mobility rate of, 43; assignment to schools, 11; attendance rate, 160, 173, 187; as commodities, 52; full-time equivalent (FTE), 80, 104, 124; percentage of voucher students, 136; race/ethnicity of, 156, 160, 162, 203n5, 204n7; with special needs, 27

suburban schools, 77, 192n3

suspensions/expulsions, 160, 173, 187

Tamarack Community School, 26

taxpayer surveys, 3, 20, 151, 158–63; accountability guidelines and, 169–76; gathering/dissemination of information and, 163–67

teachers, 22, 98, 172, 177, 191n3:2; interaction with parents, 52, 57; Milwaukee survey of, 48–58; number of, 23; parents' knowledge about, 156, 159; political effects of competition and, 47; public school, 181; qualifications of, 99, 116, 117, 120, 160, 173; ratio to students, 204n7; reporting of change by, 54–58; salaries, 139; work lives of, 63, 66–67

teachers' unions, 2, 60

Teske, Paul, 47, 100, 112

test scores, 6–7, 10, 16, 99, 156; accountability guidelines and, 173, 174, 187; as information about schools, 161; systematic reporting of, 22

Texas Bufkin Academy, 27, 140

textbooks, 139

Thompson, Tommy, 12, 15, 121

tuition costs, 23, 136, 171

Twenty-seventh Street School, 71–72

uniforms, 103, 116

Urban Day School, 30, 31, 35, 141, 202n4; cumulative percent of voucher enrollment, 36; enrollment increase at, 32; number of voucher enrolled students, 34

vandalism, 114

vouchers, 3, 4, 10; academic achievement and, 8; academic research panel and, 148–49; accountability and, 14–18; eligibility requirements, 13–14; funding mechanisms for, 122–32, 185–86; grade level and, 39–40; mechanism of, 137–38; number of students using, 23, 24, 26, 27, 33, 35, 119; qualification for, 102; targeted program, 12–14; taxpayer support for, 152–54; tuition costs and, 171

Waldorf School of Milwaukee, 25, 26

Washington, D.C., 6

Wells, Amy Stuart, 47

Westside Academy, 71

whites, 13, 49, 168; accountability guidelines and, 170, 171; information requirements and, 162; parent survey and, 83, 89; taxpayer surveys and, 153, 154

Williams, Annette "Polly," 12, 15, 16, 134

Wilson, James Q., 111

Wisconsin Department of Public Instruction (DPI), 7, 9, 10, 16; budget of, 17, 126, 200n2; data published by, 23; fiscal accountability and, 122, 127, 129; information made available by, 105; Internet

databases of, 188; school closures and, 28; school expenditures and, 134; teacher database, 48; voucher eligibility and, 14
Wisconsin Knowledge and Concepts Exams (WKCE), 68–71, 174, 196n10

Witte, John, 7–8, 77, 81–82
Woodson Academy, 30, 31, 32, 34, 36, 144

Yeshiva Elementary School, 141, 144

Zebaoth Learning Center, 25, 28